The Poles

919.8
P
c.1
1399

Copyright © 1988, Raintree Publishers Inc.

Translated by Hess-Inglin Translation Services

All rights reserved. No part of this book may be reproduced or utilized in any form or by any means, electronic or mechanical, including photocopying, recording, or by any information storage and retrieval system, without permission in writing from the Publisher. Inquiries should be addressed to Raintree Publishers Inc., 310 West Wisconsin Avenue, Milwaukee, Wisconsin 53203.

Library of Congress Number: 87-28697

1 2 3 4 5 6 7 8 9 0   91 90 89 88

Printed and bound in the United States of America.

Library of Congress Cataloging in Publication Data

The Poles.

(Science and its secrets)
Includes index.
Summary: Focuses on life at the North and South poles, the animals that flourish there, and the past and future of the Arctic and Antarctic.
1. Polar regions—Juvenile literature. [1. Polar regions] I. Series.
G587.P65   1988   919.8   87-28697
ISBN 0-8172-3078-5 (lib. bdg.)
ISBN 0-8172-3095-5 (softcover)

THE POLES

Raintree Publishers — Milwaukee

Contents

The Earth and Its Poles

Have the continents always had the same shape?	6
How were the poles formed?	8
Does the North Pole resemble the South Pole?	10
Are there seasons?	11
Does the Midnight Sun shine through the night?	12
Are there volcanoes at the poles?	13
Where do icebergs come from?	14
Are icebergs the same at the two poles?	15
What is the difference between a seal and a sea lion?	16
Why are whales hunted?	17
How do polar animals resist the cold?	18

The North Pole

Map of the Arctic	20
What are the arctic lands?	21
Does arctic ice move?	22
Which kinds of fish are found in the Arctic Ocean?	23
What kinds of birds are seen?	24
Are there walruses at the two poles?	25
Where does the polar bear live?	26
Where did the musk ox originate?	27
Are there still wolves in the Arctic?	28
Have some animals become extinct?	29
Where do Eskimos come from?	31
How were they able to tolerate the cold?	32
What are their boats like?	34
How do Eskimos hunt?	36
How is an igloo built?	38
Are there still sled dogs?	39
Is there Eskimo art?	40
Do you want to learn some Eskimo words?	41
Who first discovered the Arctic?	42
Who rediscovered Greenland?	43
What are the Northeast and Northwest Passages?	44
Who was the first to arrive at the North Pole?	46

The South Pole

Map of the Antarctic	48
What are the Antarctic lands?	49
Why is it hard to tell the difference between auks and penguins?	51
What other birds are in the Antarctic?	52
Are there seals in the Antarctic?	53
Who discovered the Antarctic?	54
What did Commander Charcot discover?	54
Who was Ernest Shackleton?	56
Who was the first to arrive at the South Pole?	58
What bases are present in the Antarctic?	60
Glossary	62
Index	64

Have the continents always had the same shape?

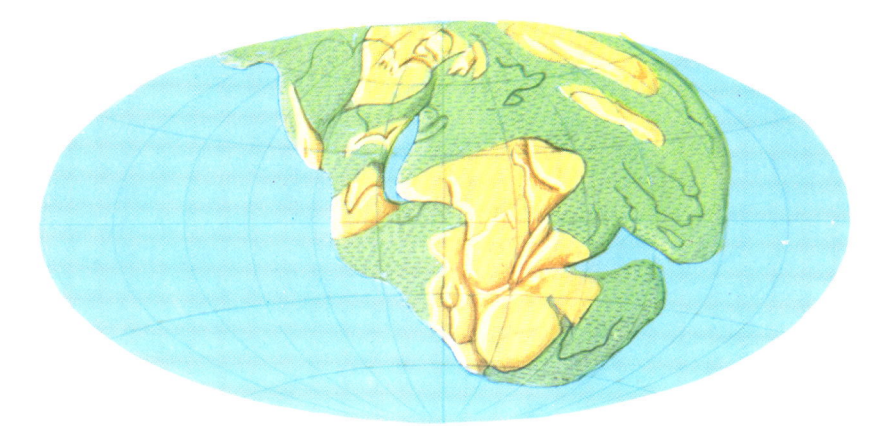

300 MILLION YEARS

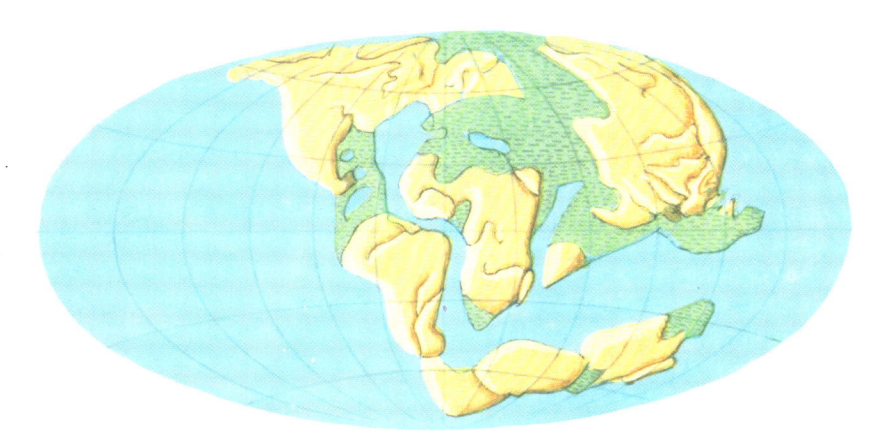

80 MILLION YEARS

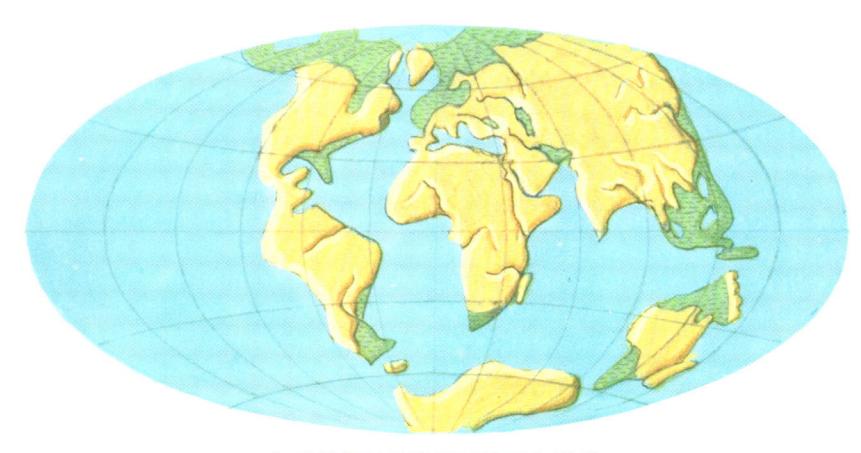

1 MILLION YEARS

If you look closely at this map, you can follow the formation of the continents. Top: "Pangaea" (one continent). Center: The breakup of the land mass. Bottom: Finally, about one million years ago the continents began to take on the shapes that they have today. 1 - North America, 2 - South America, 3 - Eurasia, 4 - Africa, 5 - Australia, 6 - the Antarctic. The green areas represent shallow oceans which covered certain areas of the continents.

No, they have changed often since the beginning of the world...

The earth formed 4½ billion years ago. The continents were formed much later. Scientists' calculations show that four hundred million years ago they formed only one continent called Pangaea, surrounded by only one ocean called Panthalassa.

One hundred million years later, this enormous block of land began to break up. First, it broke into two parts—Gondwana to the south and Laurasia to the north. Then it broke into several pieces which little by little became positioned as they are today. Is the conclusion that the continents moved? This is what the German scientist Alfred Wegener claimed in 1915 in his theory known as "continental drift."

Professor Alfred Wegener, the father of the "continental drift" theory and head of the German expedition to Greenland in 1930.

Continental Drift

Continents, like oceans, rest on "plates," huge rigid sections of the earth's crust. The plates push against one another or pull away from one another. This is caused by the action of internal forces in the earth.

For example, India, Australia, and the Antarctic continent, having separated from Africa, moved from each other one by one. The plate which India rests on drifted toward the north and slid beneath the plate of Asia. The result was an enormous fold—the chains of the Himalaya Mountains! And this action has not finished. Even today, the Himalayas grow each year by several inches.

We live in a world in perpetual movement, in countries which rest upon plates sliding like immense rafts. The plates that the two American continents rest upon move away from each other at the speed of over three inches per year. When they move quickly, terrible earthquakes occur like the one which devastated San Francisco in 1905.

The Himalaya Mountains. It is the sliding of the plates of the earth's crust which created the sudden appearance of these gigantic mountains.

How were the poles formed?

The glaciation of the Arctic

Two and a half million years ago, Antarctica was already completely covered by ice, while in the Arctic the ice had only started to form. One million years later, the high glaciers of Greenland were linked together and covered completely with an ice cap. During the hundred thousand years which followed, ice accumulated on the high regions of North America and Eurasia, and then extended down to the plains. It was the beginning of the ice age which occurred, during four periods, over the last nine hundred thousand years. These periods were called, in chronological order, Günz, Mindel, Riss, and Würm.

Pictured are two different views of the Bering Strait, the isthmus which linked Asia to North America for fifty million years.

When we speak about the "North Pole" or the "South Pole," we generally think of the entire region surrounding the actual pole.

Strictly speaking, "pole" is the point where the imaginary axis around which the earth is rotating would pass through the earth's surface. The North Pole is a point whose latitude is 90° north. The South Pole is another point whose latitude is 90° south.

But usually when we speak of the "North Pole" or "South Pole," we mean the regions which surround them.

The Arctic through the ages

Four hundred million years ago, the North Pole was in the middle of the Panthalassa, the only ocean. Greenland was connected to the northern regions of North America and Europe.

Approximately 160 million years ago, the lands of Laurasia (the northern regions of Pangaea) came closer together around the North Pole. Greenland moved away from Canada, then away from Europe one hundred million years later. North America and Asia were then united at the Arctic by a huge plain, Beringia, for the next fifty million years. As the terrestrial masses continued to drift during the last glaciation, the borders of the Arctic Ocean became as we know them today.

The formation of the Antarctic continent

At the time of Gondwana (the southern region of the Pangaea) and Laurasia, the South Pole was probably in the present eastern region of Antarctica, close to what is now Madagascar. Antarctica was then attached to Africa, Australia, and India.

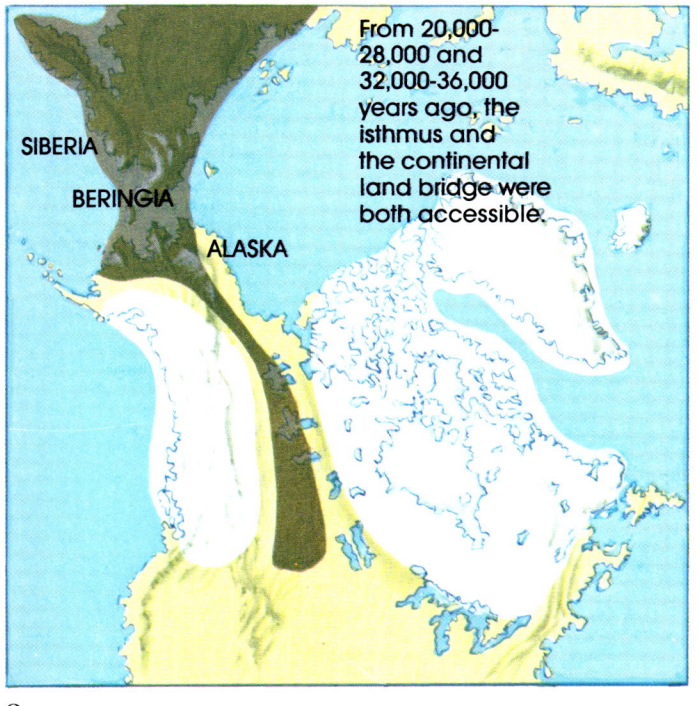

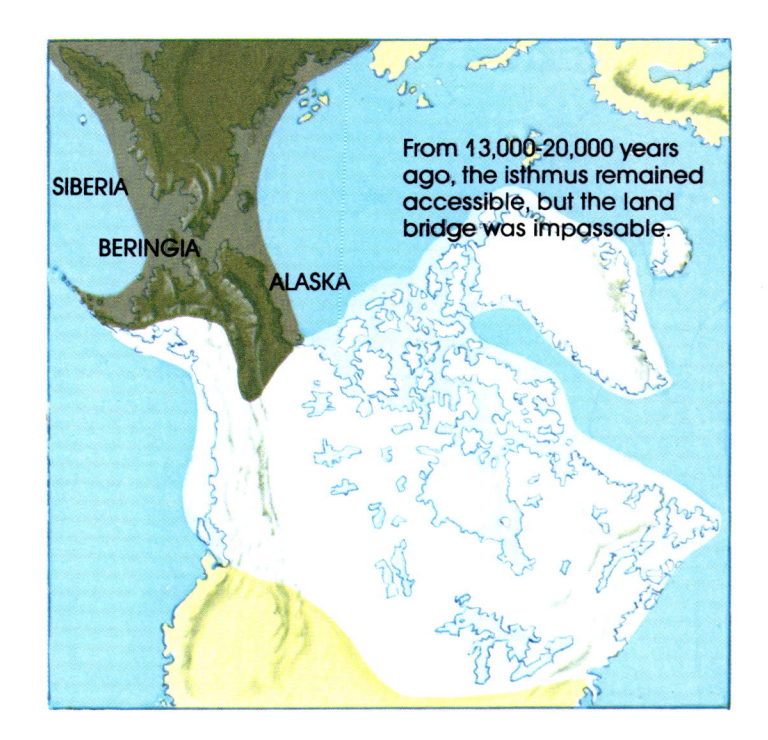

From 20,000-28,000 and 32,000-36,000 years ago, the isthmus and the continental land bridge were both accessible.

From 13,000-20,000 years ago, the isthmus remained accessible, but the land bridge was impassable.

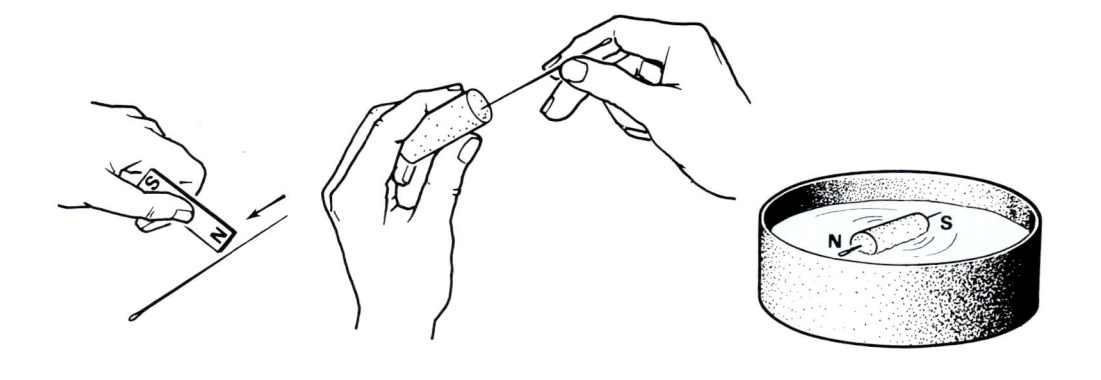

To build a compass yourself, rub the tip of a needle with the "north pole" of a magnet. Pierce through a cork with this needle. Place the cork in water. The magnetic point of the needle will point south. The opposite direction is north. The compass ranks as one of the original "great discoveries" because of its aid to navigation.

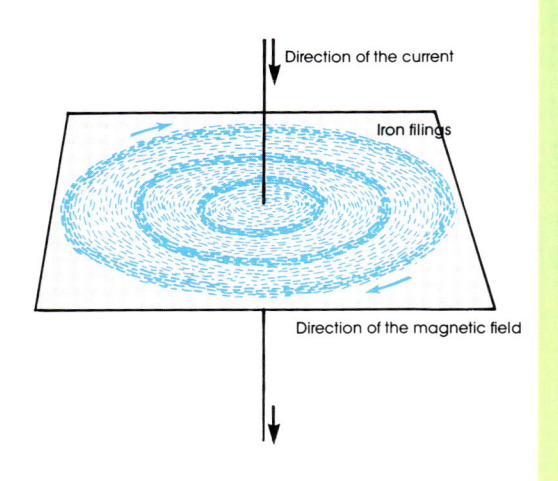

The magnetic poles

The earth can be compared to a huge magnet because it creates a magnetic field around itself. You can learn to recognize magnetic fields by pouring iron filings on paper and by moving a magnet underneath the paper. The earth's magnetism is produced by electricity coming from the core of the earth. The magnetic poles have, as in a magnet, a magnetic north pole and a magnetic south pole. But they should not be considered the same as the geographic North and South poles because they are not at the same place. The north magnetic pole is at present near the Boothia Peninsula to the northeast of Hudson Bay. The south magnetic pole is next to Adélie Land, the French area of the Antarctic.

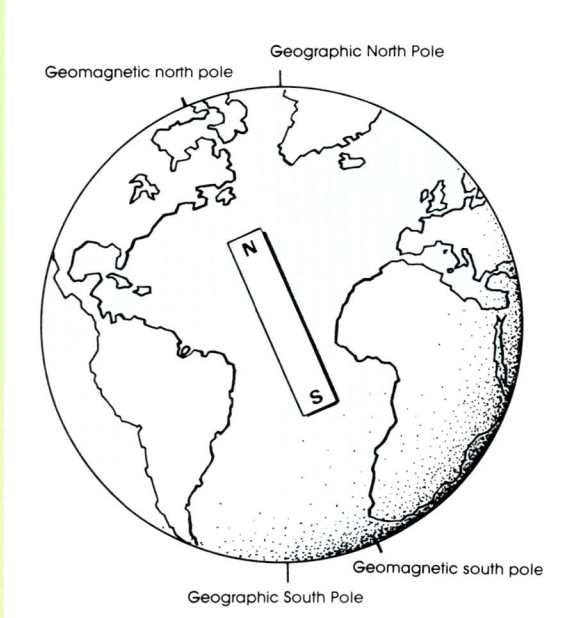

Approximately 160 million years ago, huge lava flows spread over the whole of Gondwana and over what would become Antarctica. It is the sign of a great, final disassociation. Antarctica (which begins to appear) will be separated from Australia, but it will take one hundred million years. These two continents drift independently, the Antarctic continuing its movement toward the South Pole. Twenty million years ago, glaciation spread everywhere. Two to three million years ago, the glacial antarctic lands and ocean froze and remain so today.

The Greenland ice cap. Four hundred million years ago, this large island was attached to the coasts of North America on one side and to the coasts of Europe on the other.

Does the North Pole resemble the South Pole?

Yes and no. Yes, because it is cold and there is snow and ice. No, because there are many differences.

First, the North Pole is in the middle of an ocean—the Arctic Ocean—while the South Pole is almost in the middle of the Antarctic continent. The Arctic Ocean extends over a depression 9,843 feet (3,000 meters) deep, while the Antarctic continent has the shape of a dome which rises to more than 9,843 feet (3,000 m). Yes, the distance is the same, but in the other direction!

Another difference is that the Arctic Ocean is surrounded by inhabited lands while the Antarctic has always been desolate. The only life found at the South Pole is marine, while at the North Pole there are many varieties of land mammals.

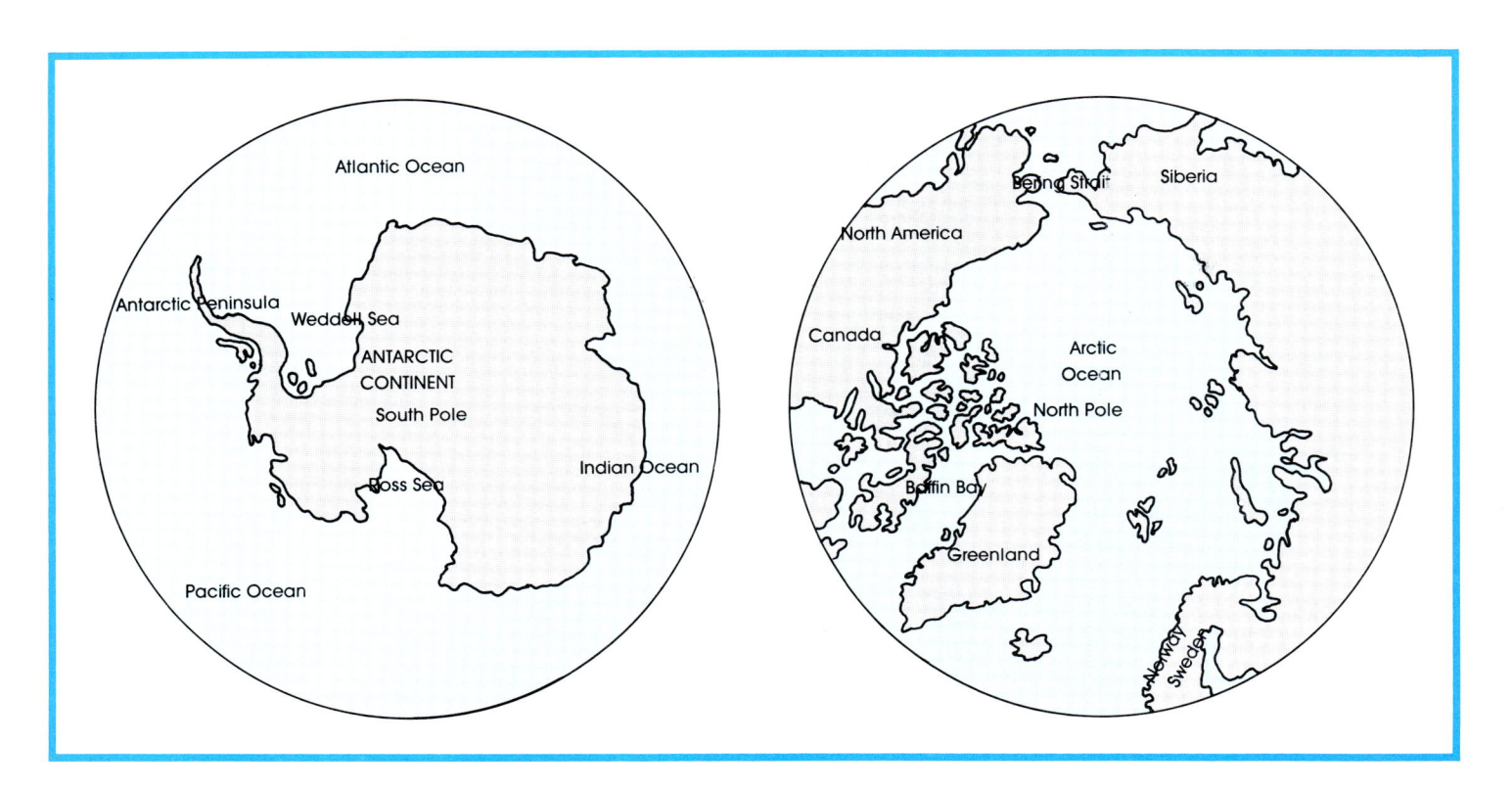

These two maps show one difference between the North Pole and the South Pole. The Antarctic is a continent covered with ice and surrounded by oceans, while the Arctic is an ocean surrounded by land.

Charcot said...

"If, one day, you are lost at one of the poles without knowing which one, there is a sure way to know how to recognize which pole. If you find yourself face to face with a polar bear, you are at the North Pole because there are no polar bears in the Antarctic. If you find yourself face to face with a penguin you are at the South Pole because there are no penguins at the Arctic."—*Jean-Martin Charcot*

Comparisons

The Arctic Ocean, which is bordered by North America and Northern Eurasia, has a surface of 3,662,200 square miles (9.5 million square kilometers). It is the smallest of all the oceans. The continent of Antarctica has a surface of 5,100,000 square miles (14 million sq. km), which is approximately four times the size of Western Europe.

Are there seasons?

Since spring and fall are almost nonexistent at the poles, it can be said that there are actually two main seasons—a very long winter and a very short summer.

In the Arctic lands

The passage from winter to summer is marked by the breakup of the ice floes and the melting of the snow. Then it is summer. In many places, the ground appears. But soon, it starts to snow again. In the summer, the Eskimos can live in tents and hunt and fish. But during the winter, the risks of freezing or starving to death are great.

At the other end of the globe

In the Antarctic, winter lasts eight to nine months. Then the breakup of the great ice floe which surrounds the continent begins. This is followed by a maximum of three months of summer.

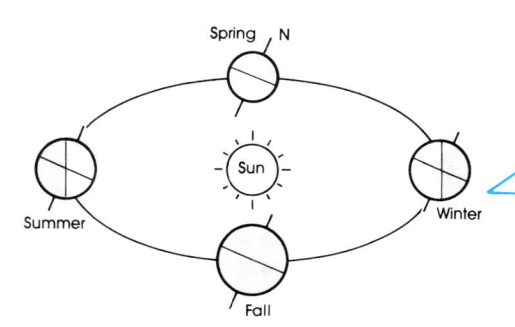

The earth, by revolving around the sun, also rotates around itself on an axis whose end points are the two poles. This axis is tilted on the "plane of the ecliptic," the path of the sun through the sky.

What is a *white-out*?

A *white-out* is the name for the terrible icy fog which forms at high speed when the conditions of atmospheric humidity are favorable for it. Huge white-outs can form in minutes! Imagine what it's like: At first, visibility is good, the sky is gray, the surface of the snow is white, you can see the horizon. And then suddenly... you see nothing... nothing at all, not even for a few feet! This phenomenon is the terror of pilots (helicopters in particular).

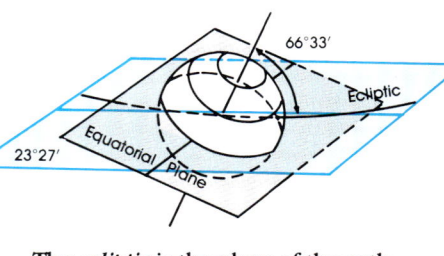

The *ecliptic* is the plane of the path of the sun through the sky during the year. The *obliquity* of the ecliptic is the angle (about 23°27′) that this plane makes with the angle of the equator. It is because of the positioning of these two planes that there are alternating seasons.

Watch out for blizzards!

The blizzard is an essentially polar phenomenon—snow elevated by violent winds. A blizzard can extend 33-330 feet (10-100 m) vertically. The visibility is almost zero, creating a critical situation.

This photograph was taken in the middle of a blizzard!

The ice floe

An ice floe includes all of the ice which covers the polar seas. Ice that covers land is called an ice cap. The ice floe or pack is composed of two types of ice. The *annual ice*, which is formed at the beginning of the winter season, can be several feet thick. It is broken up in the spring—called the "debacle"—and drifts with the currents and finally melts. The *polar ice*, which remains from one year to the next, maintains a constant thickness. These two kinds of ice have the shape of flat rafts and constitute what are called floes. In some places, huge blocks of ice as big as mountains that come from glaciers join the ice floe.

Does the Midnight Sun shine throughout the night?

The polar circles

The Arctic Circle is an imaginary line that runs through parts of Canada, Alaska, Russia, and Scandinavia. The Arctic Circle marks the edge of an area where the sun stays above the horizon one or more days each year. The sun does not set there on the longest day in summer, and the sun never rises there on the shortest day of winter. The Antarctic Circle forms the northern boundary of Antarctica. To the south of this circle, the nights and days are reversed when compared with the Arctic.

Yes, this marvelous sun of the polar regions does shine the whole night through—but not for the whole year and not at the two poles at the same time! The sun shines at midnight at the Arctic Circle on June 22. The periods of midnight sun last longer farther north. In northern Norway, which is called "The Land of the Midnight Sun," there is continuous daylight from May through June. The sun does not set for six months at the North Pole. This occurs between approximately March 21 and September 21.

There are twenty-four hours of sunlight on December 21 at the Antarctic Circle. The midnight sun shines at the South Pole between September 21 and March 21.

The midnight sun is caused by the tilting of the earth toward the sun. First the South Pole and then the North Pole face the sun as the earth travels around the sun. While one polar region faces the sun, it has continuous daylight. And at that same time, the opposite pole is in continuous darkness.

Are there volcanoes at the poles?

Yes. When the ground is frozen, it sometimes allows liquid lava to shoot upward and out through cracks in the earth's crust.

Today, most of the volcanoes in the polar regions are extinct.

In the Arctic
Between Greenland and the far north of Norway, there is a volcanic island, Jan Mayen, which is a part of Norway. Its summit, Beerenberg, is still active. Its last eruption was in 1972.

There are also undersea volcanoes in the Arctic Ocean.

In the Antarctic
The only two volcanoes still active in the Antarctic are Erebus on Ross Island, and the volcano of Deception Island in the Antarctic Peninsula. A lava lake boils at the bottom of Erebus crater, but there have been no eruptions since James Ross discovered it in 1842. The volcano of Deception Island, on the contrary, erupted several times during the twentieth century. The volcano erupted again recently, forcing the three small English, Chilean, and Argentinian bases at the bay to evacuate their staffs.

The Midnight Sun. This beautiful luminous cross comes from the reflection and the refraction of the sun's light on the small ice crystals in the atmosphere.

Right: The Erebus Volcano. Ice towers are situated on the high slopes. *Top:* An enormous bubble 33 feet (10 m) wide is about to burst under the pressure of the volcanic gas.

Where do icebergs come from?

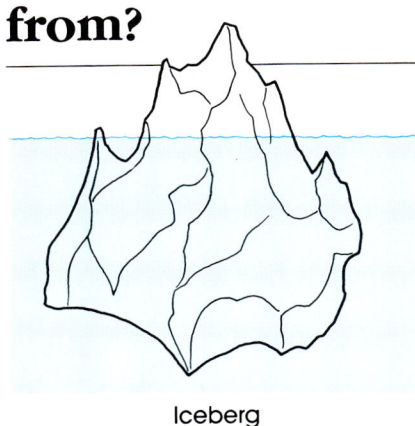

Iceberg

Notice the extent of the submerged mass.

Ice floes and icebergs are not the same. An ice floe is formed from sea ice, while icebergs (mountains of ice) are made of land ice.

Hidden danger

Approximately nine-tenths of the volume of an iceberg is hidden underneath the sea. Icebergs form where chunks of ice break away from a glacier as it flows into the sea. The sun and wind melt the top of an iceberg. The bottom, which is underneath the water, melts much more slowly. The top melts away. The bottom of an iceberg is very dangerous to ships that do not realize it is there.

When it snows in some polar regions, the snow is transformed little by little into ice. This ice is fluid and flows in the direction of the greater inclination, as a river would do, but much more slowly. When the ice flows toward the lowest altitudes between the chains of mountains, it forms glaciers or rivers of ice. If these glaciers move all the way to the ocean, the "fronts" which detach become icebergs.

Since snow is nothing but frozen rain (water in the form of ice), the icebergs are really great mountains of frozen water.

Compare the icebergs of the Arctic *(below)*, having irregular shapes and "cathedrals" of ice, with the flat icebergs of the Antarctic *(right-hand page)*.

Are icebergs the same at the two poles?

In general, they are very different.

The torturous icebergs of the Arctic

They are created by glaciers which flow down to the sea, but these glaciers overflow only rarely into the sea. Their "tongues" and their fronts usually stop at the beach. That is why they are much more varied in their shapes than the icebergs of the Antarctic. Beautiful cathedrals of ice generally do not arise in the Antarctic Sea.

The tabular icebergs of the Antarctic

On the contrary, most of the gigantic icebergs of the Antarctic have a regular shape, a flat surface which makes us think of the shape of a table. They are often called "tabular" icebergs.

They are created by the collapse of the fronts of great glaciers and ice shelves. They are much bigger than those of the Arctic, and they flow down to the sea where their "tongues" float for dozens of miles. This explains their table-like shapes. The same is true for ice shelves which have separated. The greatest tabular icebergs come from these ice-shelves, while those with irregular surfaces with ridges come from glaciers.

The world's largest icebergs

There are many icebergs in the Arctic, but the biggest icebergs are in the Antarctic. The greatest ever observed was discovered in 1956 by the American ice breaker ship, *Glacier*. The iceberg was 208 miles (335 km) long and 60 miles (97 km) wide, which is bigger than Belgium!

Read the text carefully to discover which of the photographs on this page contains sea lions.

What is the difference between a seal and a sea lion?

There is more than one difference. You may have seen, at the circus or on television, a sea lion balancing a ball on its nose. A lot of people think that it is a seal, but it is not. A seal would not be able to do that. Out of the water it is heavy and slow and moves with difficulty. Also, it is not as intelligent as the crafty sea lion.

To recognize a sea lion at first glance, look to see if it has ears. They are not big, but they are visible. The seal's ears are hidden.

Another difference is that these two animals do not swim the same way. The sea lion uses its front flippers to swim in the water, and the hind flippers are used like a rudder. The seal propels itself by the movements of its front flippers (similar to fish with their fins). Its two other flippers are stretched alongside its body. The sea lion can run on the ground while the seal moves by jolts of its body.

Seals and sea lions are numerous in the Arctic and the Antarctic.

16

Why are whales hunted?

These enormous sea mammals are great treasures for hunters, who hunted them for centuries. As a result, the species almost disappeared!

Fortunately, an international commission on whale hunting was established in the twentieth century to control the activity of the whalers. After Henry Hudson's discovery of whales in the Arctic Ocean in the seventeenth century, Russian, Norwegian, Dutch, and French whalers began hundreds of years of whale hunting.

In the Antarctic Sea, on the contrary, whales lived a long time without being attacked by hunters because the continent was only discovered in approximately 1820. But today, despite laws and the efforts of many countries against the slaughter, the Russian and Japanese boats hunt the whales as if no laws existed.

These modern whalers have very efficient techniques—detection radar, explosive harpoons, and helicopters. Their whaling boats are actual factories weighing fifty to sixty thousand tons.

Hunting is a crime when it threatens the survival of a species.

What products come from whales?

Not one ounce of the 150 tons that a whale can weigh is lost. Most importantly, whale oil is used to make lubricants, glycerine, soap, margarine, beauty creams, paints, varnishes, cosmetics, and a complete range of chemical and industrial products from candles to linoleum. From the liver of the whale, the pharmaceutical industry extracts medicine rich in vitamins and hormones. The bones are used as fertilizers, and the bowels are used as food for cattle. Whalebones have even been used as umbrellas.

The beluga whale, also called the white whale, is found in the Arctic and is usually 10-23 feet (3-7 m) long.

Greenland seal.

What are the temperatures at the poles?

By far the coldest continent, Antarctica has had temperatures in winter from -76°F (-60°C) to -126.9°F (-88.3°C), which is the world's lowest recorded temperature. Midsummer temperatures may reach as high as 59°F (15°C). Average winter temperatures in the Arctic are -30°F (-34°C) in the north to -20°F (-29°C) in the south. Summer temperatures are low, generally below 45°F (7°) with occasional intervals of 65°F (21°C).

Is the earth getting cooler?

Geophysical drilling in Greenland allowed scientists to foresee as early as 1965 a general cooling trend for the earth. Fifteen years later, the layer of snow and ice has increased by about seven percent. The southern limit of the icy arctic winds (upon which a great part of our climate depends) has moved southward by several hundred miles. The changing climate is a phenomenon that anyone can notice if he or she is old enough to compare the climate of twenty years ago with the climate of today.

How do polar animals resist the cold?

When you are cold in bed, what do you do? You add another blanket or two. By doing so, you multiply the layers that protect you. Plus, between each blanket, there is air. It is the best insulator there is!

Nature takes care of everything...
Nature gave polar animals the same system of successive layers. During the winter, the polar bear, the polar fox, the wolf, the caribou, and the seal possess a thick layer of fat under their skin. The seal's winter layers can reach a thickness of more than 4 inches (10 cm). Insulation against cold weather is insured by the layer of fat, the skin, and the hair.

Some animals have even more complete protection because they also have a layer of down. For example, the eider, an arctic bird, has down which is used to make warm, cozy eiderdown quilts.

To avoid the loss of body warmth, nature provides some animals with supplementary protection. The legs of bears and polar dogs have hair between their toes. The temperature of the paws of these animals is much lower than the rest of their bodies.

The polar fox. The small size of its ears helps it to avoid heat loss.

THE NORTH POLE

Kamandorskiye
Kurilskiye
Aleutian Islands
Pacific Ocean
Kamchatka
Sakhalin
Bering Sea
Sea of Okhoisk
St. Lawrence Island
Gulf of Alaska
Anchorage
Bering Strait
Mt. Mckinley
Kotzebue
Ambartchik
Alaska
Fairbanks
Canada
Point Barrow
Wrangel Island
Eastern Siberia Sea
New-Siberia Islands
Beaufort Sea
Tiksi
Port Radium
Coppermine
Uranium-City
Banks Island
Siberia
Victoria Island
Pr. Patrick Island
Laptev Sea
Arctic Ocean
Pr. of Wales Island
Magnetic North Pole
Taymyr
U.S.S.R.
North Pole
Hudson Bay
Devon Island
Southhampton Island
Ellesmere Island
Franz Josef Land
Thule
Labrador
Baffin Island
Baffin Bay
Novaya-Zemlya
Kara Sea
Upernavik
Fort Chimo
Jakobshavn
Spitzberg
Barents Sea
Davis Strait
Greenland
Godthab
Greenland Sea
Murmansk
Frederikshab
Angmagssalik
Jan Mayen Island
Julianehab
Tromso
Arkhangelsk
Finland
Arctic Polar Circle
Iceland
50°F (10°C) Summer Isotherm
Reykjavik
Leningrad
Norway
Sweden
Greenwich Meridian
Helsinki
Atlantic Ocean
Oslo

Pictured is the Angara River in the Soviet area. On this Siberian river, one of the greatest dams of the world was built.

What are the arctic lands?

They are the lands which surround the Arctic Ocean. Starting with northern Europe and proceeding counterclockwise, there you will find a large part of northern Siberia, the northern part of Alaska, a large part of Arctic Canada, and all of Greenland.

How is the Arctic defined?

The Arctic is the area surrounded by a line drawn through all northern locations with an average summer temperature of 50°F (10°C). This line is known as the 50°F (10°C) summer isotherm. What is an isotherm? It is the line drawn by connecting sectors having identical temperatures. The 50°F (10°C) summer isotherm in the warmest month is a line drawn by connecting sectors having temperatures of at least 50°F (10°C) during the warmest month of the year. The arctic lands are lands which are situated to the north of this isotherm.

To which countries do these lands belong?

The arctic lands are divided into sectors. They each have a triangular shape with their summits touching the North Pole. By starting from Scandinavia, first you will find the Norwegian sector which is comprised of Spitzberg or, more precisely, the Svalbard archipelago. Next is the Soviet sector which goes as far as the Bering Strait. Then there is the sector belonging to the United States, which covers all of Alaska. Then comes the Canadian sector, which stops at the channel which separates Ellesmere and Greenland. Lastly, between the Canadian sector and the Norwegian sector, there is the Danish sector, which covers Greenland.

21

Does arctic ice move?

What is the thickness of the ice?

The depth of the icecap in Greenland was measured by French scientists during various expeditions. They made a map of the underground rock. The average thickness of the ice is 9,843 feet (3,000 m) and the maximum is 10,499 feet (3,200 m).

The ice fields flow like liquid over the ground, and the ice floe is carried by the sea current.

A snowflake's journey

A glacier is nothing but an outpouring of ice. The icecap in Greenland is not a glacier. It is a dome of ice in which the different particles of ice also move. For example, a snowflake which falls in the center of Greenland, from an altitude of about 9,800 feet (3,000 m), will sink little by little under the weight of other flakes which will fall after it, year after year. Transformed into ice, it will start to slide toward the exterior to appear again inside an iceberg. If it slid to the west, it might end up in Baffin Bay. If it slid to the east, it might end up in the Greenland Sea. This sliding will take nature several hundred thousand years.

The drifting of the ice

The ice floe of the Arctic Ocean is also in perpetual movement. The ice which composes it generally turns counterclockwise around the North Pole. However, some of the floes drift southward, pushed by the Labrador currents. Others drift with the streams along the east coast of Greenland to its southern tip.

A glacier in Alaska. It looks like a solidified river, but it flows.

The drifting of the *Jeannette*

This American polar ship, *Jeannette*, was ice bound not far from the Bering Strait in September, 1879. In June, 1881, after twenty-two months of drifting, it was crushed by the ice floe and sank. In 1884, Eskimos discovered a wreck on a floe south of Greenland. It was the wreck of the *Jeannette* which had been carried by the polar current through the Arctic Ocean and along the east coast of Greenland. In 1896, the great explorer Fridtjof Nansen remembered the drifting of the *Jeannette* and decided to reach the North Pole by letting his ship the *Fram* simply drift. But the ship drifted southward, so Nansen tried to walk to the pole. He told his companion that "after all, the distance to the pole was only as far as the distance from Paris to Marseilles." Needless to say, he never reached the pole on this very dangerous journey.

Above left: Capelins drying on the beach. *Above right:* "Fletan" fishing at Thule, Greenland, through an opening in the ice.

What kinds of fish are found in the Arctic Ocean?

The salmon trout, which is a typical Arctic fish, feeds on small fish common to this region called capelins.

The capelins resemble the smelt and live in such dense schools that the surface of the water wriggles everywhere for miles. They are obviously the delight of thousands of birds, seals, and whales, which eat them by the ton. Eskimos catch capelins with a net.

The "fletan" is abundant, especially in Baffin Bay. It is a flat fish which has its two eyes on the same side of the head, like a sole. This is because it swims flat, always on the same side, and the bottom eye is no longer useful.

In the depths, there also exists a dogfish which is not very well known —the greenland shark or blue skin shark. It can be 16-20 feet (5-6 m) long. The Eskimos catch it to feed their dogs and for the oil in its liver.

A fish which cannot stay still

The cod very accurately follows changes in temperature. In the beginning of the century, it was found near the Iceland coasts, then it was found off Newfoundland, then along the western coasts of Greenland. Today, it is again located off Newfoundland. Why all this movement? Because it needs water at 39°F (4°C).

What kinds of birds are seen?

Auks, petrels, cormorants, sea gulls, great skuas, terns—they are in the arctic sky by the millions.

Although they both have the same white and black plumage, the auk should not be mistaken for the penguin, which is a bird of the Antarctic. Auks are excellent divers, and they have narrow and short wings which allow them to swim in shallow water. In the air, on the contrary, they are not so clever!

The arctic tern is probably the bird which travels the farthest in one year—from the Arctic to Antarctica and back!

The great skua is a feared bird of prey. It attacks the terns to devour them or to force them to give up the fish they have.

It would be nice to study the great auk, a superb bird of the Arctic in the last century. But it no longer exists. Hunting has made the great auk extinct.

A colony of auks.

Are there walruses at the two poles?

No, they are only found around the Arctic Ocean. None are found in the Antarctic.

Walruses are especially numerous in the Bering Sea. They are enormous creatures. The males can measure as much as 16 feet (5 m) long and weigh half a ton! The males have tusks which are, in fact, very strong teeth. They grow continuously. If one breaks, it grows again! They can reach 24 inches (60 cm) in length and are probably used to plow the bottom of the sea in order to remove shells that they then crush with their teeth. That is why the walrus is sometimes called "the animal which walks with its teeth."

But don't believe that this *pinniped* (mammal with four flippers) eats just anything. Thanks to its tongue, lips, and powerful mustache, it is able to obtain only the best food available.

Walruses go on land only to warm themselves in the sun or to mate.

Male walruses live in herds. This, unfortunately, makes them an easy target for hunters.

Where does the polar bear live?

This superb but dangerous plantigrade animal (walking on the sole with the heel touching ground like people) lives on an ice floe. Polar bears can live their entire lives on the ice without ever touching land. Polar bears are exclusively carnivorous and hunt seals.

It is not a teddy bear!

The polar bear is extremely dangerous, and this cannot be stressed enough. Like every beast, it attacks if it feels it is in danger. It will also attack if it is hungry or wounded. Females may need to attack to protect their cubs.

The polar bear is a solitary creature. The mating season is short. Frequent battles between the males occur during this time. Since the polar bear was hunted without regulations, it has been on the protected species list for the past several years.

An adult polar bear may be as tall as 9½ feet (3 m) and weigh as much as 1,000 pounds (450 kg).

The polar bear has a smaller head, longer neck, and is more slender than other bears. This type of body makes polar bears powerful and agile swimmers.

At one time threatened with extinction, polar bears are protected today. In the last century, Eskimos hunted them with knives.

A herd of musk oxen. Notice the thickness of the coat, perfectly suited to the arctic climate.

Where did the musk ox originate?

The musk ox came from Asia and lived over a vast surface. In the past, musk oxen bones have been found in the United States and in Europe. Drawings representing it have been found on the walls of prehistoric caves, especially in France.

Musk oxen have been hunted to a great extent, and they are seen today only in the far north of the American arctic and in northern Greenland. They live in herds and feed on grass, willows, lichen, and other small plants.

The musk ox is no taller than a small cow. Its shoulders contain a big hump of muscles. Its musk odor at mating time resulted in its name. The long, shaggy, dark-brown hair of the musk ox falls onto the ground. Underneath it is a down of exceptional quality—the thinnest, the softest, the warmest of all the downs in the world. The warm down is appreciated by the Eskimos who call it *krouviout*.

Which side has more courage?

When a herd of musk oxen feel they are in danger, they group together forming a square. The males are on the outside, facing all directions. The hunters of the last century said there is no animal more senseless since they are easy targets when they group themselves this way. The hunters, however, are the senseless ones.

On this stone, a musk ox was carved by a prehistoric artist thousands of years ago.

Are there still wolves in the Arctic?

Of these two wolves with beautiful fur, only the white one is truly from the Arctic. Nature wanted to protect it from hunters and other prey by giving it the color of the snow.

Yes, but the wolf is a hunted animal.

The wolf is sometimes thought of as nasty and cruel. It is, on the contrary, a timid animal which should inspire kindness. It is similar to a dog. It is probably the dog's ancestor.

The wolf lives in a family. It is its familial organization which makes it the most evolved animal of all the mammals. When a male wolf chooses a female, it is for life. This love and fidelity extends to the young, too, who are attached to their parents even after having built families of their own.

Bloodthirsty, the wolf? Far from it. It eats only small rodents—squirrels and field mice. When the rodents are not sufficient, only then does the wolf hunt larger animals (most often caribou). But, as with all predators, the wolf attacks only sick, crippled, or old animals. By eliminating these types of animals, wolves perform an important natural function.

The "big bad wolf" exists only in tales...

You should know that the wolf never kills for pleasure but out of necessity. It lives intelligently with all the animals of its territory. Wolf families will sometimes cross a herd of caribou without causing the least panic among them. The caribou seem to know that the wolves will not attack just for the sake of attacking.

Have some animals become extinct?

Unfortunately, yes. Here are two very sad stories about arctic animals that have become extinct.

The Steller's sea cow

They were Sirenians or plant-eating mammals who lived in the water. They were very large, from 16-20 feet (5-6 m) long. They weighed about nine thousand pounds. Steller's sea cows lived in large numbers off the islands near Kamchatka in Siberia. They were discovered in 1741 in the Bering Sea and were massacred by the hunters, who were quick to exploit their fat which had the extraordinary taste of butter. Twenty-five years after their discovery, the Steller's sea cows were extinct.

The great auks

These handsome birds, which were about two feet (60 cm) tall, had atrophied wings, which means they were no longer useful to them. They stood vertically and walked with difficulty on land. In the sea, they swam very well. There were millions of them in the Arctic.

But as early as the sixteenth century, sailors began hunting them ... with hatchets! Salted and dried, they were used as food, and their thick skins were used as fuel. A whole great auk, correctly dried, was an excellent torch to light one's way! On June 4, 1844, the last two were killed.

Two types of animals that have been hunted to extinction are the great auk *(above)* and Steller's sea cows *(below)*.

Where does the word *Eskimo* come from?

It probably comes from the Indian word *Kree eskimawak* (raw meat eater). The French missionaries transformed this word. They wrote *esquimau*, in the plural form *esquimaux*, and in the feminine form *esquimaud*. Today, *eskimo* is used.

Where do Eskimos come from?

America was unpopulated for a long time. Fifty thousand years ago, the Bering Strait did not exist. In its place there was Beringia which, according to the fluctuation of the oceans, could reach up to 930 miles (1,500 km) wide. It was by this route that the Asiatic populations passed, pursuing the animals chased from their meadows by climatic changes. The first migration was the migration of the ancestors of the Indians.

The ancestors of the Eskimos

A reheating of the earth occurred, and the ice melted. Beringia was under water, and the Bering Strait appeared. The migrations stopped.

About ten thousand years ago, Beringia came out of the water again, and people started once more to move toward better hunting grounds. These were the ancestors of the Eskimos. But they were not lucky. They did not find a passage toward the south and found themselves cornered between the frozen Arctic Ocean and the ice cap which covered the whole of North America. It is between this frozen water and this icy land that they emigrated little by little toward the east. They adapted their lives to the conditions that nature imposed upon them.

A Canadian Eskimo *(left)* and a Swedish Lapp—two very different types of individuals.

The Lapps and the Eskimos

Many people confuse the two. There is no relationship between them. The Lapps are Finno-Ugrians—parents of the Finnish, the Hungarians, and especially the Turks. The Eskimos come from Asia. The former live in northern Europe, the latter in Alaska, Canada, and Greenland.

What is an *Inuk*?

The Eskimos call themselves *inuit*. It is the plural of the word *inuk*, which means man. Eskimos were isolated from the rest of the world for a long time without knowing if other people existed anywhere else.

How were they able to tolerate the cold?

At home with the Eskimos—softening a seal skin *(right)*; a young girl wearing her summer *kamiks* or *boot-pants* *(far right)*.

Below: Two hunters with polar bear fur pants and caribou skin coats.

The Eskimos succeeded in living on polar lands because of the civilization they developed, one of the most astonishing civilizations in the world.

They used all that nature gave them (which is not very much) to solve their problems—rocks and pebbles, snow and ice, and animals like seals and caribou.

With such resources, these people succeeded in creating a habitat which protects them from storms and cold, a way of dressing themselves to suit the climate, and various means of transportation.

The secrets of the Eskimos' clothing

Because of contact with outside civilization, most of the Eskimos are forgetting their traditions, which is a pity. But it was not long ago that they dressed and lived exactly as their ancestors did.

They wore seal or caribou skin clothes. The clothing allowed air to circulate between the different layers because the Eskimos had discovered that air was the best insulation against the cold.

They still wear jackets called *anoraks* or parkas. They wear two jackets—the first one close to the skin with the hair inside, while the second one has its fur outside. The layer of air circulates between the two. The same is true for the pants.

Kamiks are the boots. They are made of seal or caribou skin, and sometimes from polar bear skin. When the skin is stripped, tanned, and oiled, it is for the summer months. When the fur is kept on, it is for the winter. Between the outer sole and the inner sole, a layer of grass is placed. The grass is dried during the summer. It makes excellent insulation, and it is easy to replace.

The polar explorers imitated the Eskimos in their way of dressing, and it was that which allowed them to bear the cold and to discover an unknown world.

A bear skin on display and waiting to be sold. Fur trade is prosperous in the Arctic, but it is more profitable for the commercial buyer than for the Eskimo hunter.

What are their boats like?

The kayak is not always a one-seater...

In some regions, kayaks (Eskimo canoes) are big enough to carry the whole family. It is fun to watch the arrival of these boats. First, only the shape of one person is seen in the entrance hole. We believe he or she is alone. But when the kayak docks, the rest of the group appears. Perhaps another adult and one or more children will come into view. They have been lying down inside the kayak with their noses to the deck!

The Eskimos use two kinds of boats—the *kayak,* now adopted almost everywhere in the world to go down river rapids, and the *umiak.*

The *kayak*

This frail canoe is united with the person who slides into its entrance on top, like a finger in a glove. Not everyone is capable of using a kayak because it is necessary to fold the knee slightly backward. This ability is usually only acquired as a result of special training from an early age. The kayak and its occupant are like one object. The slightest movement of the person is transmitted to the kayak and vice versa.

It is thanks to this union that the Eskimo kayaker can face wind, snow, and ice which frequently overturns the boat. Sometimes the kayaker is turned upside down in the water. If, at this time, he or she would leave the kayak to take refuge on some floating ice, it could mean being lost or freezing to death. The kayaker, therefore, needs to know how to return to the upright position while still in the canoe. The Greenland kayakers, who are the best, know forty ways to succeed in this spectacular maneuver!

The *umiak*, the family boat

This long boat resembles a whale boat and can hold up to thirty people with their belongings—tents, bags and buckets, products from the winter hunt, and the dogs. Generally, the women row while a man holds the tail rudder.

How are kayaks and umiaks made?

Kayaks and umiaks are made of a wooden frame over which sealskins are tightened. In the past, the wood was from trees cut in Siberia and carried by the currents of the Arctic Ocean to the coasts of Greenland, where they beached. But today, the wood is bought at the village store! Once the frame is finished, they take tanned, fatted, undried sealskins and fasten them over the wood. The once supple skins eventually dry and tighten on the frame.

On the left-hand page: An Eskimo hunter has attached a white fabric screen to the front of his kayak so as not to be seen by seals.
Above: Women sew sealskins which will be tightened over the wooden skeleton of a kayak.
To the left: The umiak, the family boat, has almost disappeared today. It is being replaced by European style wooden boats.

35

How do Eskimos hunt?

What did the Eskimos eat?

In the past, Eskimos ate seal or caribou meat, generally boiled in seawater. When the season allowed, they added watercress or bilberries. The vitamin C which they lacked was provided by the skin of the narwhal or of the whale. This skin is called *matak*. It is hard like rubber.

Hunting is second nature for Eskimos. They are quite skillful in this activity, which for so long occupied the greatest part of their lives.

Hunting with kayaks

In the summer, Eskimos go hunting in kayaks. In the past, they killed seals with harpoons. Today, they use guns. It is necessary for a hunter to act quickly. If the animal is killed, it may sink and disappear. If it is merely wounded, it may flee. That is why the Eskimos shoot the seal at very close range, enabling them to harpoon it immediately. The tip of the harpoon stays in the body of the animal. It has a long rope attached to it so that the seal can be recovered if it sinks or tries to flee. Hunters place a screen of white fabric at the front of the boat, which makes the seal think the boat is drifting ice! In winter, hunting is quite different.

Hunting near the breathing hole

The seal is a mammal that has to breathe air. That is why during the winter, when ice covers the water, seals make breathing holes in the ice. Hunting near the breathing hole is easy for the hunter. But it does require patience when sitting in the cold. The Eskimo sits on a small sled at the edge of the hole. When the seal comes to breathe, he harpoons the seal with a thin stick.

Once harpooned, the animal flees underneath the ice, pulling with it the long rope which is attached to the point of the harpoon. The seal is pulled back to the surface by the hunter.

Yesterday and today

In the past, winter hunting was practiced in a very unusual way. The hunter disguised himself as a seal! He was completely dressed in tanned seal skins and would advance toward his prey by crawling on the ice, grumbling and scratching like the seals do, until he was close enough to throw his harpoon. This type of hunt is still practiced today, but with a gun.

Below: Caribou hunting. *On the right:* Two kinds of hunting—harpooning and hole fishing through the sea ice.

Hunters cut up a walrus after the kill.

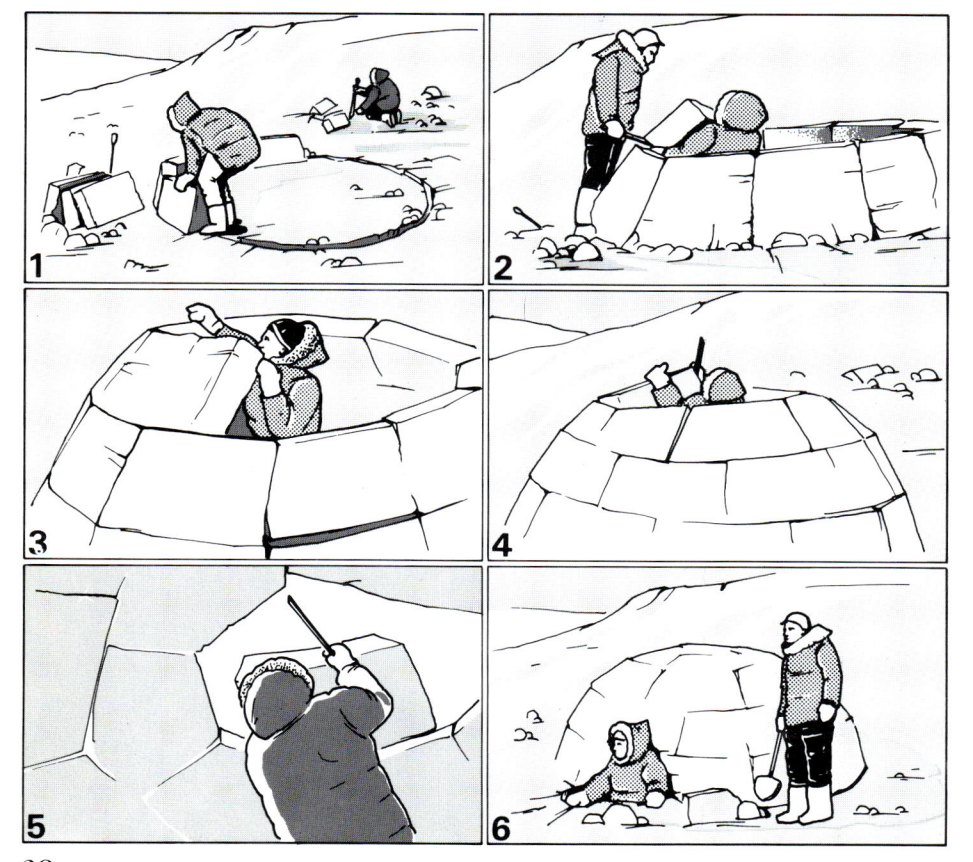

How is an igloo built?

The word *igloo* does not mean snow house or ice house but simply "house." Only the Eskimos of northern Canada built, and still build, such shelters.

How is an igloo constructed?
The main necessity is a flat surface of snow well packed by the wind. Eskimos probe the snow with a stick that they drive into the ground. If no resistance is encountered, the snow is good. Then, blocks of this snow are cut. Each block is about 2-3 feet (61-91 cm) long and 1-2 feet (30-61 cm) wide. They are cut with a snow knife. In the past, the knife was made of bone. Today, snow knives are made of metal.

The inside of the igloo is built at the same time as the outside. A first circle of blocks, already angled to form the inward shape of the igloo, is firmly set on the snow's surface. An angled side is cut the length of three or four blocks. This side will be the beginning of the spiral along which all the other blocks will be placed. The last one in place will give solidity to the whole construction.

When the last block is put in place, where do you think the builder is? Inside! He or she has to cut an opening to get out!

The phases of igloo construction

(1) Positioning of the first snow blocks. *(2)* Positioning of the blocks which have to follow the inclination of the first ones. *(3)* At the same point as the photograph *(above)*. *(4)* It is almost finished! *(5)* An Eskimo works from inside the igloo. *(6)* The Eskimo has to cut out an entrance so that he can exit!

Are there still sled dogs?

There are fewer and fewer sled dogs. The time when Eskimos used dog sleds to travel is gone. Today is the reign of the snowmobile. And for long trips, Eskimos use airplanes.

However, these beautiful dogs, which were so useful to the polar explorers, are still numerous in some areas. For example, they can be found in the small town of Jakobshavn on the west coast of Greenland. They are used for hunting during the winter on the ice floe. They are also used to revive local color... pulling sleds of tourists!

Eskimo dogs

The Eskimo dog originates in the Arctic. The category includes three pure breeds—the Eskimo breed, the Alaskan malamute, and the Siberian husky.

The three types possess certain common characteristics. They all carry their tails curled high to keep them free of ice and snow. Their coats are made of a layer of fine hair covered by a layer of coarse hair. This allows them to stay outside and keep warm, even overnight, in bitter cold weather. They all have upright and pointed ears. The feet are large and hairy for warmth and so that the dogs do not sink into the snow. Many Eskimo dogs do not bark—they howl.

Eskimo dogs are work dogs. They pull sleds with supplies and passengers. They hunt seal, bear, and musk ox. They can pick up the scent of air holes where seals breathe.

The dogs have a tremendous amount of endurance. Stamina is neccessary to survive their stark environment. They are also courageous and have a great deal of fighting ability.

Dogs that pull sleds can travel 20-40 miles (32-64 km) per day. They can pull a large amount of weight by sled.

Below left: Sled dogs are harnessed in a precise order, based on hierarchy. There is always a leader. *Above:* Greenland dogs or Eskimo dogs. *Below:* Siberian husky.

Is there Eskimo art?

The masks from the past were inspired by religion. For example, they could represent the powers of good or evil. Today, the Eskimos have been converted to Catholicism or Protestantism, and the masks are made only for tourists.

Below: Whale hunting scenes and ritual dances carved on the jawbone of a beluga (white whale) by an Eskimo artist a long time ago.

Yes, there is art of great variety and beauty.

It is amazing that these people, who lived for so long in a cold and dangerous world, were able to produce such beautiful sculptures and carvings.

The art of the Eskimo is very old. Decorated harpoon heads which date from 1500 B.C. have been discovered. In Alaska, Canada, and Greenland, the Eskimos sculpted astonishing figures in steatite (a soft stone of the area). They also carved decorative or religious subjects on the ivory of walrus tusks or caribou antlers.

Will Eskimo art survive?

Today, this artistic activity has not stopped. It is even on the rise. Many people have discovered its beauty, and a need has been created. But there is danger that some businessmen have commercialized it without understanding the meaning of the carvings and sculptures. They are mass producing the "art" for profit.

In contact with civilization, it is hoped that the Eskimo artist will be able to retain his or her purity and inspiration.

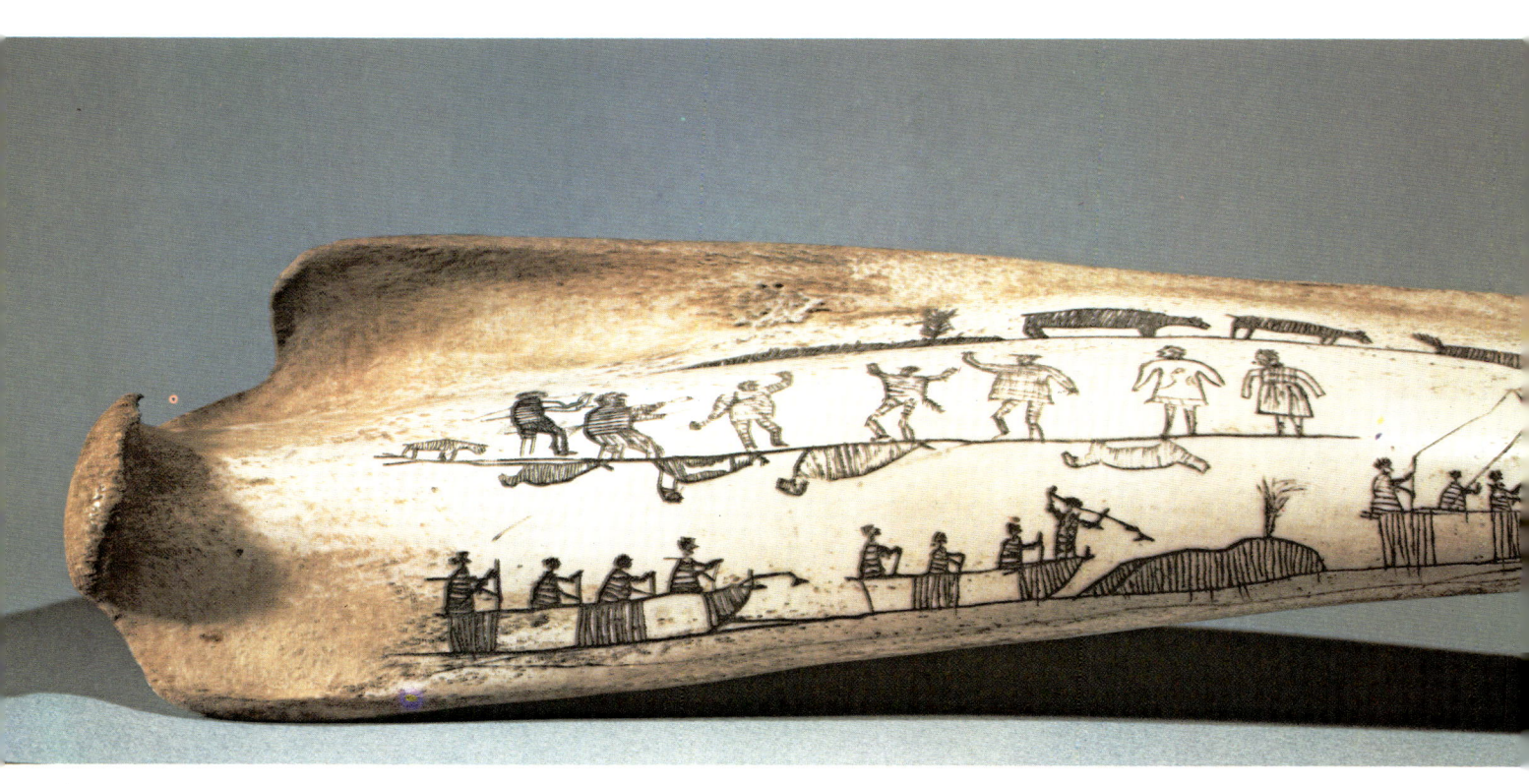

Do you want to learn some Eskimo words?

You already know *igloo*, the house; *inuk*, man; and *anorak*, jacket.

Here are others: *ipek*, the table; *nudia*, the woman; *sila*, time; *imak*, the sea; *imek*, water; *krimek*, the dog; *tutok*, the reindeer or the caribou; and *puidek*, the seal.

Is the Eskimo language an easy one to learn?

No, it is one of the most difficult languages in the world because its grammar is completely different from ours.

Many languages are made with words placed one beside the other, while Eskimo language is a language which attaches the words to each other. For example, one particular fjord is named Kanguerlouksouaksiak (written phonetically). This name is divided into several parts: Kanguerlouk, the fjord; souak, large; siak, small. It means "the not quite large fjord."

The example above is in the Greenland Eskimo language. Somewhere else, the pronunciation and even some words may be different. But globally, all the dialects are similar. People speaking the east coast Greenland language can be understood by the Eskimos of Hudson Bay, Canada, and Alaska.

Here is an example of writing in the Eskimo language invented by French missionaries for the Eskimos of Hudson Bay. The Eskimos never had their own writing.

The lands that Eskimos inhabit are shown with dots.

Do Eskimos have a religion?

Today, the Eskimos are Christians—Catholic in Arctic Canada and Protestant in Alaska and Greenland. In the past, they had their own religion. It was an explanation of the forces which people are faced with, the meaning of life on the earth, and the certainty of survival after death. The religion of the Eskimos was a collection of beliefs in supernatural forces and various things in their environment—rocks, ice cliffs, the sea, winds, etc. These forces could be beneficial or hazardous.

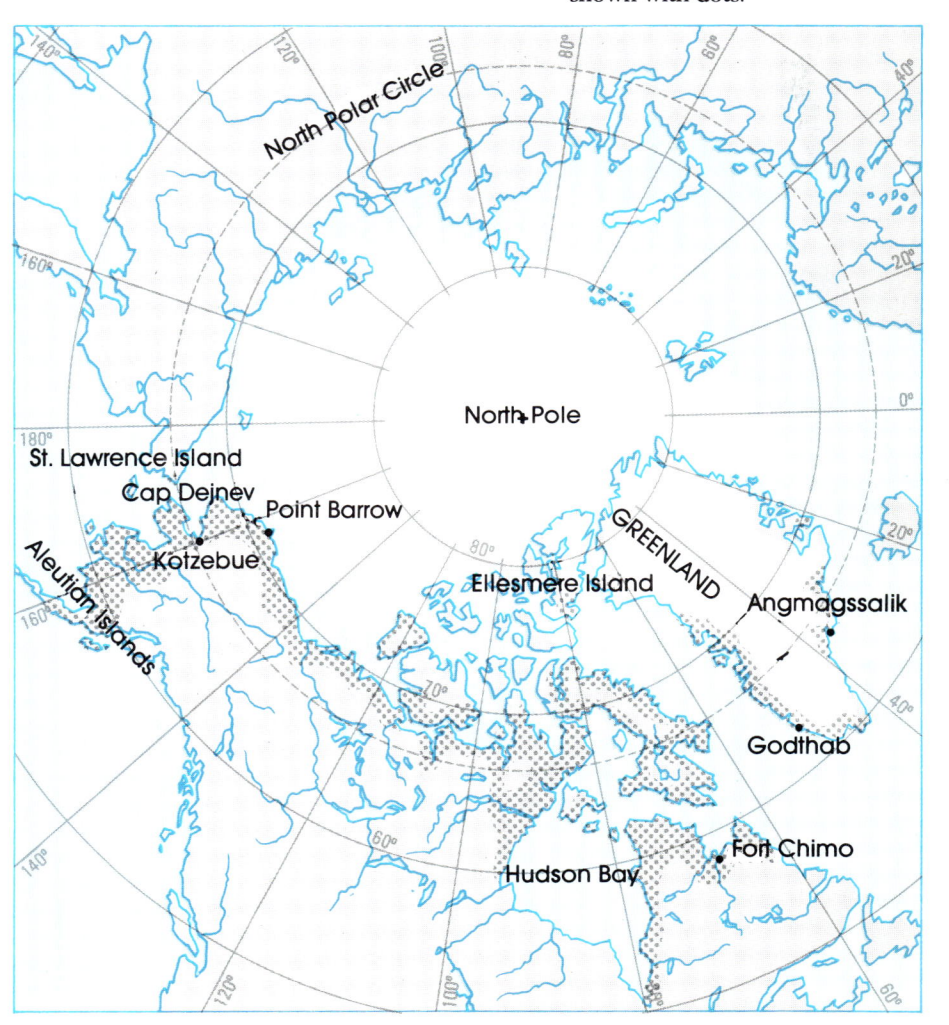

A Viking ship reconstructed by Norwegian descendants.

Who first discovered the Arctic?

The most ancient of these discoverers known was a Greek of the fourth century B.C., born in Marseille, France. His name was Pytheas.

The discovery of Greenland

He was an astronomer, a good sailor, and an adventurer. It was necessary to be so to dare going to the north to find amber, which was then very coveted. He reached a land that he named Thule. He described the area in this manner—"where nights were long, where it was cold, and where the sun and the sea were joined, sometimes in one gray mass." Maybe it was Iceland. But his story seemed so unbelievable that he was called a liar.

However, it has been demonstrated that he really did go to the Arctic and that his description corresponded to the truth!

Erik the Red

Next, the Vikings discovered Greenland and America. It is now believed that the Vikings were the first to discover America and not Christopher Columbus. In 983, Erik the Red, Viking chief from Norway, was forced to leave Iceland because his violent temperament made him undesirable. Sailing toward the west, he went around the ice floe toward the south and landed in an unknown place—Greenland.

Years later, his son, Leif Eriksson, was carried off course by a storm while headed for Greenland. He landed on the American coast in approximately the year 1000.

Who is the patron saint of the polar explorers?

It is St. Brendan. In the sixth century, he went to the Arctic to find paradise. When he came back, he said that he had seen cathedrals of opal and emerald crystals (the icebergs). He said that he had landed on a very small island, where he made a fire to cook his meal. Once the meal was finished, the island started to move. He and his crew just had time to flee before they saw the island swim away. It was a whale!

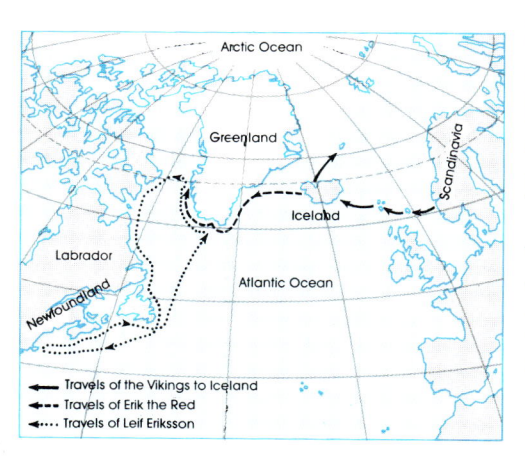

Who rediscovered Greenland?

For several centuries, colonies of Vikings settled on the western coasts. Eventually, these settlements disappeared, and Greenland was forgotten. In 1585, the Englishman John Davis rediscovered it by landing on its western coast. Further exploration of the coast came much later because it was difficult to reach. It was blocked during the winter by a solid ice floe and dangerous during the summer because of the drifting of this ice floe. It was in 1884 that the Danish Gustav Holm discovered the Eskimos of Angmagssalik, the last ones of pure race.

The first coast-to-coast crossing via the ice cap

This crossing was accomplished in 1888 by the Norwegian Fridtjof Nansen. Since that time, many expeditions have crossed the desert of ice in Greenland at different latitudes.

Since 1948, there has been systematic exploration of the largest island in the world.

This is a map of the most important expeditions to Greenland.

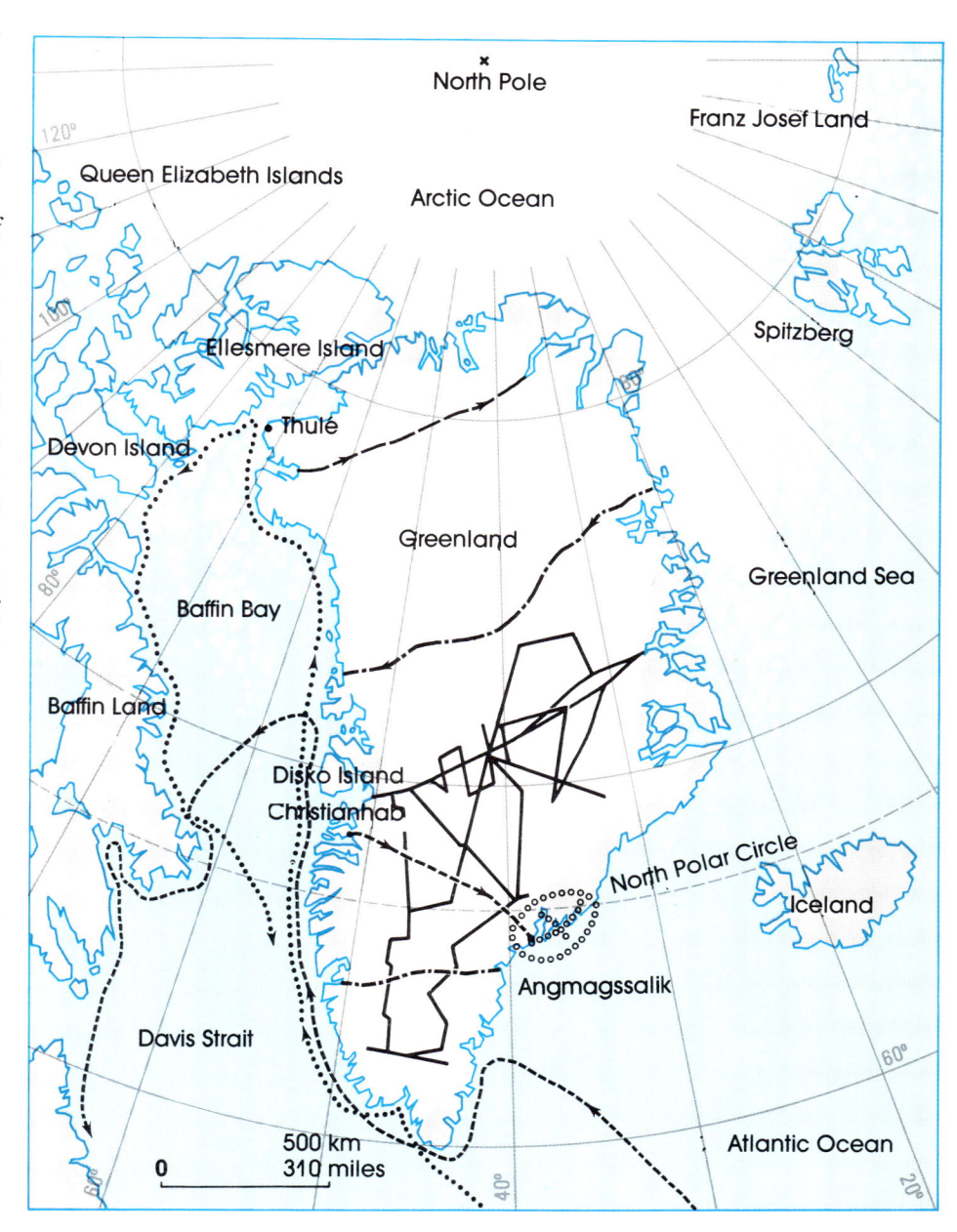

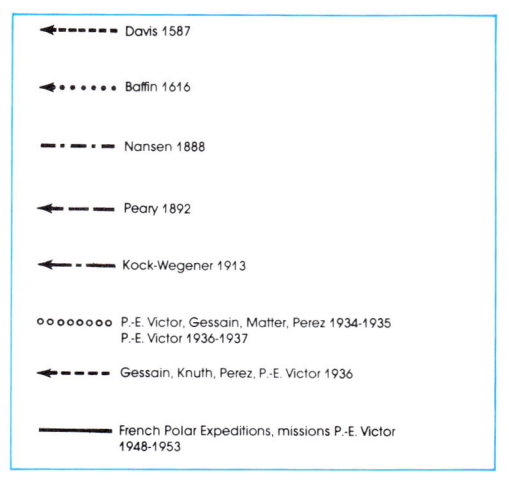

Legend:
- Davis 1587
- Baffin 1616
- Nansen 1888
- Peary 1892
- Kock-Wegener 1913
- P.-E. Victor, Gessain, Matter, Perez 1934-1935 / P.-E. Victor 1936-1937
- Gessain, Knuth, Perez, P.-E. Victor 1936
- French Polar Expeditions, missions P.-E. Victor 1948-1953

Captain Charcot

From 1926-1936, the *Pourquoi pas?* ("Why not?"), a ship of the French National Navy, made (with Charcot as head of the missions) annual cruises to the Greenland Sea. On September 16, 1936, the boat was wrecked during a storm on the reefs north of Reykjavik. Out of the forty-four people on board, only one was saved. The government gave a national funeral to Charcot and his companions.

What are the Northeast and Northwest Passages?

These are maritime passageways that sailors, since the sixteenth century, have tried to find for commercial reasons. Why? Because traders had to make the long journey across Asia with their caravans to bring rare products such as spices and silk back from the Orient. It was the famous "silk route." Then, people began to think that one or several channels probably existed which would allow passage to China by boat through the polar regions. These were the Northeast Passage to the north of northern Europe and Siberia, along the Arctic Sea; and the Northwest Passage to the north of Arctic America, through the Canadian islands.

The Northeast Passage is crossed!

At last, after long and unsuccessful journeys attempted by different countries, the Swedish baron A.E. Nordenskjöld launched an expedition. He left Norway in 1878 with two ships—the *Vega* (a three-masted boat) and the *Lema* (which was somewhat smaller). On September 27, stopped by the ice, Nordenskjöld decided to pass the winter in Kouliuschkin Bay, 124 miles (200 km) west of the Bering Strait. The target was almost reached. On July 18, 1879, the *Vega* continued on its route, passing the strait two days later and arriving at Yokohama, the Japanese harbor, on September 2.

The Northwest Passage is no longer a dream!

Throughout the nineteenth century, there were many expeditions, none successful. Then, in 1903, on a small ship called the *Gjoa,* the Norwegian Roald Amundsen left with six men aboard.

Roald Amundsen, the great Norwegian explorer.

After having reached icy Baffin Bay, he had to make a course through the various channels of the Arctic islands. He had to stop and pass the winter. It was the same the next year. His boat was blocked by the ice.

In August of 1905, the boat was at last able to proceed. But again, the expedition had to pass another winter. Finally, on July 13, 1906, the *Gjoa* was freed. On August 30, the ship crossed this difficult passage that, for four centuries, so many sailors had dreamed of conquering.

The midnight sun on the summer ice floe (Baffin Land). The winter ice plates are called *floes,* and the lakes and rivers which are between them are *polynyas.*

Who was the first to arrive at the North Pole?

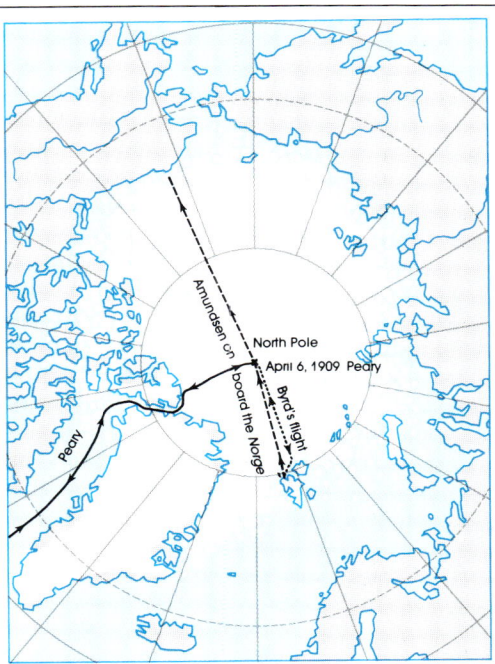

A French newspaper humorously illustrated the controversy between Cook and Peary.

Peary and his dogs on board the *Roosevelt,* the expedition's ship.

History tells us that it was the American Robert Peary who was the first to arrive at the North Pole. He reached it on April 6, 1909, with four Eskimos and his faithful companion, Mat Henson, who had participated in all his expeditions for twenty-five years.

But this great event was disputed.

Dr. Frederick Cook, who had been the doctor on several Arctic and Antarctic expeditions, affirmed that he reached the pole on April 21, 1908, one year before Peary!

The violent controversy which followed remains unresolved today.

Many people believe that both of them reached the North Pole and that Frederick Cook was probably the first. Unfortunately, because the box with all his instruments, his notes, and his calculations disappeared, he was never able to prove anything. The Danish commission which was responsible for the research said, "It has not been proven that Cook reached the North Pole, but neither has it been proven that he did not reach it."

The first flight over the North Pole

On May 9, 1926, the American Admiral Richard Byrd flew over the North Pole with his companion, Floyd Bennett. Two days later, the *Norge,* a dirigible piloted by the famous Italian engineer Umberto Nobile, took off with Roald Amundsen aboard. The plane flew over the Arctic Ocean, passing over the North Pole. On May 14, 1926, the plane landed at Teller, about 56 miles (90 km) from Nome, Alaska.

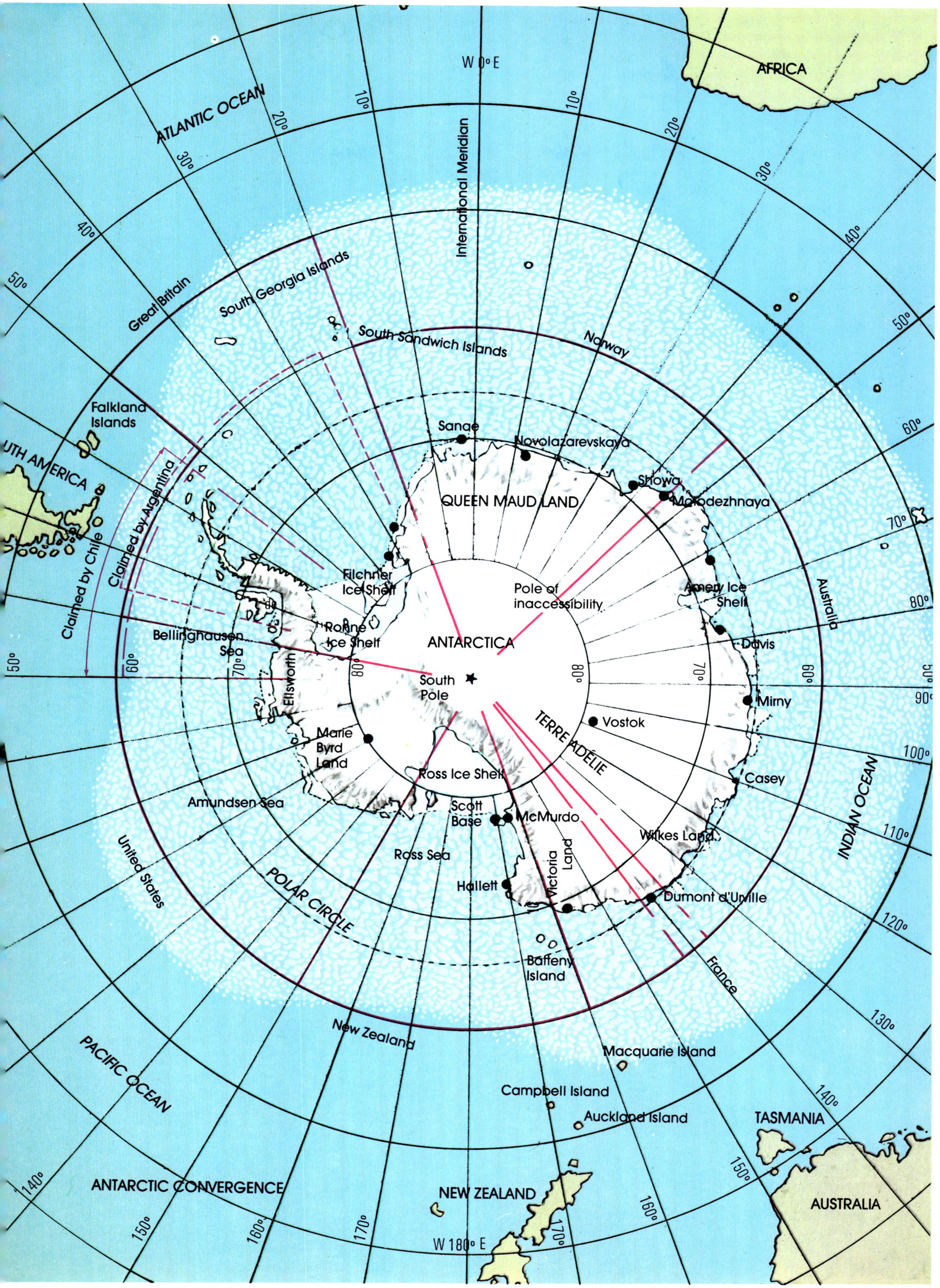

W 0° E
AFRICA
ATLANTIC OCEAN
International Meridian
South Georgia Islands
Great Britain
South Sandwich Islands
Norway
Falkland Islands
UTH AMERICA
Claimed by Argentina
Claimed by Chile
Sanae
Novolazarevskaya
QUEEN MAUD LAND
Showa
Molodezhnaya
Filchner Ice Shelf
Pole of inaccessibility
Amery Ice Shelf
Australia
Ronne Ice Shelf
Bellinghausen Sea
ANTARCTICA
Davis
Ellsworth
South Pole
Mirny
Vostok
TERRE ADÉLIE
Marie Byrd Land
Ross Ice Shelf
Casey
INDIAN OCEAN
Amundsen Sea
Scott Base
McMurdo
Wilkes Land
Ross Sea
United States
Hallett
Victoria Land
Dumont d'Urville
POLAR CIRCLE
Balleny Island
France
New Zealand
PACIFIC OCEAN
Macquarie Island
Campbell Island
Auckland Island
TASMANIA
ANTARCTIC CONVERGENCE
NEW ZEALAND
AUSTRALIA
W 180° E

THE SOUTH POLE

What are the Antarctic lands?

These lands were defined as the region which is south of the Antarctic *Convergence*. But don't let this term confuse you! It is only the line where the cold waters which surround the Antarctic continent meet the warm waters of the Pacific, Indian, and South Atlantic oceans. This line is so obvious that, when it is crossed, the temperature of the water falls several degrees.

The Antarctic continent and the regions which surround it can be divided into three groups:

The continental islands, whose climate, flora, and fauna are very similar to those of the continent.

The maritime islands, most of which are situated along the Antarctic Peninsula.

The periantarctic islands, which are situated between the northern limit of the ice floe and the Antarctic Convergence.

The *Nagga Dan* anchored between Jean Rostand Island and Petrel Island. In the foreground are oil barrels.

Which countries own them?

Traveling counterclockwise, there is first the large Australian sector which is subdivided by the small French area, Adélie Land. Then, there is the very large Norwegian sector. Next, covering the Antarctic Peninsula, three areas overlap each other, and three countries claim this peninsula—Great Britain, Chile, and Argentina. Next there is an unclaimed area that has no owner. Last is the New Zealand area.

How thick is the ice?

Under the continent, the average thickness is 6,890 feet (2,100 m). The maximum thickness is in the western Antarctic (the area which faces South America), and it is 14,765 feet (4,500 m) thick.

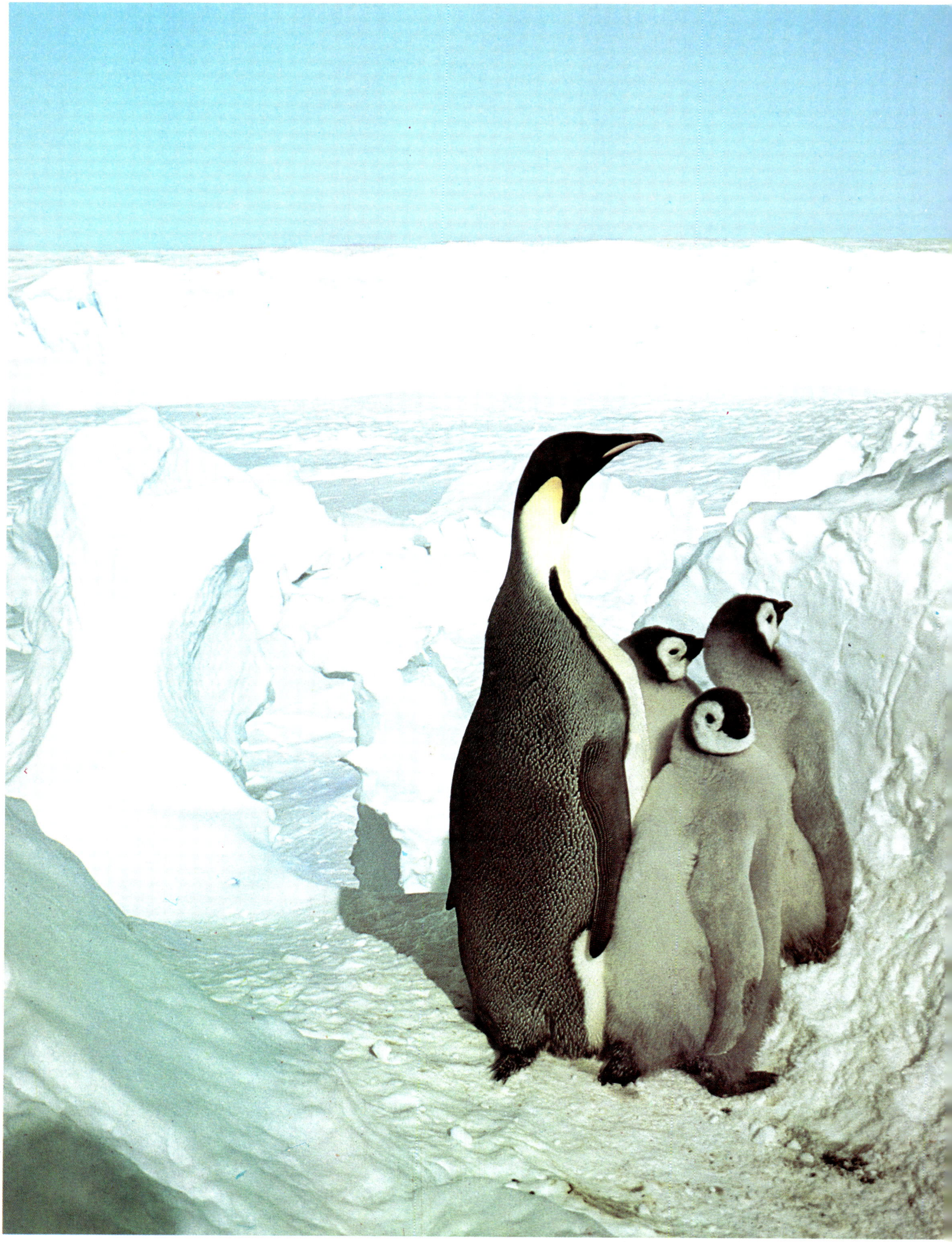

Why is it hard to tell the difference between auks and penguins?

Throughout the world, penguins are called auks because the old English sailors, seeing the penguins' black backs and their clear bellies, mistook them for the auks of the Arctic.

Birds which do not fly

Penguins are very adorable and entertaining creatures. Not very wild, they accept the approach and even the caress of people. Since they lost the use of their wings (that changed into fins) a long time ago, they move on the ground in a vertical position by walking on their webbed feet. This gives them a curious waddling motion. Some people think that penguins resemble little men dressed for a formal party.

There are many species of penguins in the southern hemisphere, but the two we find in Antarctica are Adélie penguins and Emperor penguins.

Adélie penguins

Adélie penguins are the clowns of the Antarctic. Their antics are endlessly comical. Adélie penguins lay their two eggs in a nest made of pebbles and debris, at precise spots where the couples meet every year.

The Adélie weighs about 15 pounds (7 kg) and is about 16 inches (40 cm) tall. Their main enemies are skuas and leopard seals. They breed in summer, and as many as 250,000 of them gather in a single breeding area. Several million Adélies live on the Antarctic coast.

The Emperor penguins

Emperor penguins are extraordinary birds. When winter comes, most birds of the world migrate toward warmer countries, but the Emperor penguin does just the opposite. It is the only animal in the world which goes toward the cold to multiply. Yes, it is in the middle of a blizzard in the middle of the polar night, that the female lays her one egg, directly on the ice. In the spring, the baby penguin will be strong enough to face life at the South Pole.

The size of these penguins can reach 3 feet (1 meter) in height and weigh up to 30 pounds (14 kg). The couples stay together until one of the mates dies. They meet each other every year at the same place.

Emperor penguins *(left-hand page)* breed in the harshest conditions on earth—on the icecap during Antarctic winters. Adélie penguins *(below)* of the Antarctic are the most numerous in the world.

The arctic tern flies around the world but makes its nest near the polar circle.

What other birds are in the Antarctic?

Besides penguins, there are a dozen species of birds that nest on the Antarctic continent.

They are all seabirds, from the giant petrel, whose wingspan can exceed 6 feet (2 meters), to the small snow petrel which resembles a white swallow. The albatross and the skuas also inhabit the Antarctic.

The skuas are the predators of the breeding grounds of other birds at mating time. They are sea and land birds, beautiful but vulture-like. They attack wounded adults and young, helpless chicks.

They lay only one egg and, to protect their chick, will not hesitate to attack an intruder.

The king of the migrators

The arctic tern is a very good traveler. This beautiful little bird spends the summer in the Arctic. When winter comes, it goes to the Antarctic to again find the summer. Of all the birds, it is surely the one which profits the most from sunny days! When fall comes to the Antarctic in April, it goes back to the Arctic to nest. So in one year, it tours the world!

Are there seals in the Antarctic?

Yes, there are many. They are very typical of the Antarctic.

The seals that we see most often, although they are not the most numerous (less than one million), are the Weddell seals. They were never systematically hunted because they are truly polar.

The crab seals are the most numerous (several million), but they are rarely seen on the ground because they almost always live on the high sea ice floe. Despite their name, they do not eat crabs. Their teeth form a filter similar to that of the whales. This filter allows them to retain only plankton when they feed. Plankton is the term used for all small animal and plant life in suspension in the sea that many fish and some whales eat.

The Ross seals are also seals of the ice floe. They are the least known because they are also the least numerous. It is thought that there are only fifty thousand of them.

Leopard seals can be very dangerous on the ground because, despite their awkwardness, they move relatively quickly. They are carnivorous. In the sea, they are, like every seal, very efficient. They hunt penguins which swim in shallow waters.

The king of the seals

The sea elephant is a very big seal, the largest marine animal after the whale. It can weigh up to seven tons, an enormous animal! Long hunted for its high-quality oil, the species is protected today. Sea elephants are located on islands where scientific bases are established.

Below: A male sea elephant.

Who discovered the Antarctic?

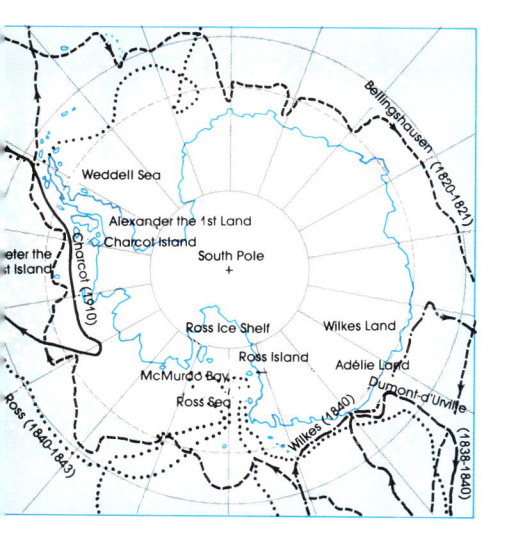

The first man to actually set foot on one of these Antarctic lands, more precisely on the peninsula, was the American Captain John Davis. He arrived via his seal boat *The Huron* on February 7, 1821. But it was after 1840 that scientific curiosity gave rise to the first expeditions.

In the race to the magnetic south pole, it was the French navy officer Jules César Dumont-d'Urville who reached the Antarctic continent as such, excluding the peninsula which extends very far north beyond the polar circle.

Then it was reached by the American Charles Wilkes, who claimed the honor of the discovery of the land which bears his name.

In 1841, the Englishman James Ross discovered two volcanoes, which he named Erebus and Terror (the names of his two ships), and McMurdo Bay. The following year, he explored the ice cliff 164-328 feet (50-100 meters) high—Ross Ice Shelf or Ross Barrier. He also discovered a large bay now known as Whale Bay.

After this series of exciting explorations, fifty years passed before there was a rebirth of interest in the Antarctic.

When was the Antarctic circled?

Baron Thadeus von Bellingshausen, as head of a Russian expedition, was the first. His ships were the *Vostok* and the *Mirny*. In 1821, he discovered Peter the 1st Island and Alexander the 1st Land.

What is an ice shelf?

It is a huge platform of ice which rests on the sea. The first ice shelf found in the Antarctic was discovered by James Ross. Its name, Ross Barrier, describes the head of this huge platform of ice and not the ice shelf itself.

What did Commander Charcot discover?

At the end of the last century and at the beginning of this century, many teams went to the Antarctic continent—the Belgian expedition of Adrien de Gerlache, the British expedition of Borchgrevink, Commander Charcot on the *Français* and the *Pourquoi pas?*

The *Français* expedition, in 1903-1905, passed alongside the west coast of the Antarctic Peninsula, which permitted its mapping. This map was, with the corrections added by the *Pourquoi pas?* expedition three years later, the only precise document for more than twenty-five years!

Charcot went again on the *Pourquoi pas?* in 1908-1910. This ship was, at the time, the most modern and comfortable of the polar ships. After having discovered Fallières Land and mapping Alexander the 1st Land, Charcot spent the winter on Petermann Island. During the summer of 1909-1910, he discovered a land to which he gave the name of his father, a famous doctor.

Commander Charcot had passed by more than 1,860 miles (3,000 km) of coasts which were until then unexplored!

Commander Charcot *(below)* and the *Pourquoi pas?* in the Antarctic *(above)* and at dock in France *(right)*.

Who was Ernest Shackleton?

Ernest Shackleton's two polar expeditions make some of the best pages of polar history.

So close to the target...

On October 28, 1908, Sir Ernest Shackleton, a British sailor, left his hut on Ross Island in McMurdo Bay with three companions. His target? —to reach the South Pole. Their sleds were pulled by the men and four ponies. They discovered an enormous glacier, Beardmore Glacier, which mounts the Antarctic plateau and traverses a gigantic chain of mountains that cuts the continent in two.

The travels of the great explorer Shackleton (1914-1916):
1. The *Endurance* is blocked in the ice.
2. Drift of the ship.
3. It sinks.
4. Drift of the crew on the ice.
5. Route with lifeboats.
6. Shackleton leaves to find help.
7. Rescue attempt.
8. Rescued!

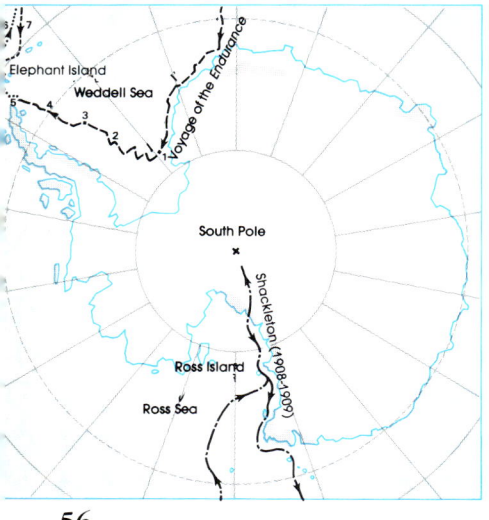

On January 9, 1909, Shackleton and his companions decided to stop. They were only 112 miles (180 km) from the pole. They had traveled 868 miles (1,400 km). They could have reached the pole, but they had only enough food for forty more days—not enough for the return journey.

So near to his goal, Shackleton had the courage to turn back to avoid risking the lives of his companions. He felt he did not have the right to gamble with their lives.

Discovering a continent!

In 1914, Shackleton left once more to try crossing the Antarctic continent by way of the South Pole. But he was unlucky again. His ship, The *Endurance,* sunk in the Weddell Sea, broken up by the ice, after having traveled 570 miles (920 km) for ten months. Then Shackleton and his twenty-six companions, taking off across the ice, tried in vain to reach land. They finally arrived at Elephant Island, an island desolate and frozen. They had not set foot on ground since December 5, 1914, one-and-a-half years!

He left the island with a few men on a boat of questionable repair to find help. The nearest help was on the island of South Georgia, 744

Above: Shown is the historical cabin of Scott and Shackleton. *Below:* During the expedition, a colony of penguins is initiated to music from a phonograph.

miles (1,200 km) away! After sixteen days of storms, cold, hunger, and exhausted by lack of sleep, they finally reached the island. But the Norwegian station was on the other side of a still unknown chain of mountains! Anyone but Shackleton would have given up. Well, he crossed the chain and required four more months and three boats before being able to rescue those who had stayed on Elephant Island.

The expedition returned to England without having lost one man.

The crossing of the continent was not achieved until 1957-1958 by a British expedition commanded by Sir Vivian Fuchs.

Who was the first to arrive at the South Pole?

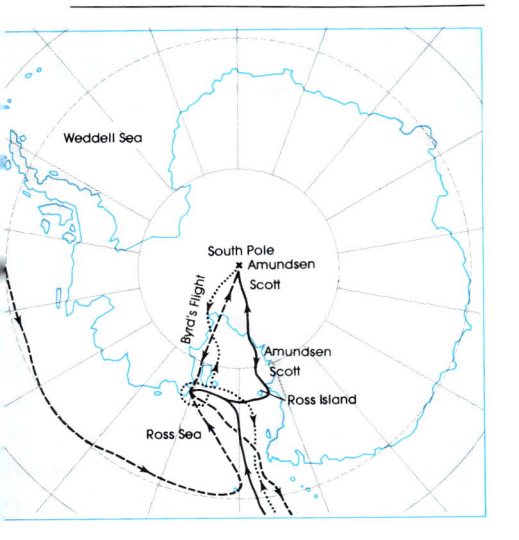

The two heroes of the conquest of the South Pole are Robert Scott (Britain) and Roald Amundsen (Norway).

Scott: a tragic end

On November 1, 1911, Scott and his team left Ross Island with nineteen horses, thirty dogs for guides, and tractor sleds which broke down very quickly.

They left food along the route to allow the assault team to come back alone if they reached the pole.

As soon as they reached Beardmore Glacier (discovered and mapped by Shackleton three years earlier), Scott sent back the second to the last help group, including the dogs, leaving only men to pull the sleds. Why not pull them with the dogs? Because Scott saw the conquest of the pole as a "victory of man over himself" and wanted his success to rest solely on his and his fellow companions' forces.

Imagine how difficult the situation became! The sleds were overloaded and the men sank into the snow up to their waists. The ice was so slippery that they could hardly stand upon it. On January 17, 1912, the expedition finally reached the South Pole, only to find a tent there flying the Norwegian flag! Yes, Amundsen had arrived one month before Scott. Scott still had to travel 930 miles (1,500 km) in frightful conditions to return to his base.

Deceived and exhausted by the terrible effort of pulling the sleds, the five men took to the return trail.

Look carefully at this historical photograph. It shows Scott and his companions arriving at last at the South Pole and discovering that Amundsen was there before them. Driven to despair, exhausted, they will all die during their terrible return trip. Next to the corpses, a roll of film was found and developed. This is one of the photographs.

The first flight over the South Pole

On November 28, 1929, Admiral Richard Byrd left by plane from his base on the Ross Ice Shelf. After having flown over the pole and refueling his plane at the foot of the mountains of the Antarctic chain, he returned to the base less than nineteen hours later.

Two died en route. Fifty-six miles (90 km) from their base, Scott and his last two companions died of starvation and exhaustion under their tent, stopped by a storm.

They were found six months later. Scott, understanding he was dying, had written several beautiful letters ... to his wife, to his son, and to England.

Amundsen—a great "first"

On October 19, 1911, Roald Amundsen got under way with four men, four sleds, and thirteen dogs.

The distance to cover was 62 miles (100 km) shorter than the route chosen by Scott. But Scott's route had already been followed by Shackleton who had carefully mapped it. Amundsen dashed straight to the south, toward the unknown.

On December 14, 1911, Amundsen's party reached the pole. They stayed there three days and pitched a tent with food and medical supplies that Scott finally found one month later.

On January 25, the expedition returned to its base with two sleds and eleven dogs. The five men had traveled 1,857 miles (2,995 km) in three months.

Admiral Richard Byrd (the third from the left) and his team during his second expedition to the Antarctic. His objective was to establish a meteorological station. He had 2 ships, 3 planes, 1 autogyro, 153 dogs, 50 sleds, 3 tractors, 3 caterpillar trucks, and ... 3 cows to assure the expedition its daily ration of milk!

What bases are present in the Antarctic?

> **What is Geophysics?**
> It is the study of the physical properties of our planet—movements of the terrestrial crust, magnetism, electricity, meteorology, and so forth.

There are many. They are used as places to live and work and as a point of arrival and departure. But it is since the International Geophysical Year (1957-1958) that permanent bases were created throughout the Antarctic continent and even on the glacial plateau.

The International Geophysical Year (1957-1958)

Half a century ago, a German scientist, Alexandre von Humboldt, decided to fill a need. In the polar regions, no observatories or scientific laboratories existed. He succeeded in establishing some of these through Northern Europe and Asiatic Russia as far as Alaska.

Then two Austrians founded the International Polar Years, which later became the International Geophysical Year.

It was an extraordinary act of cooperation between thousands of scientists from sixty-seven countries. They met for the first time in 1957.

The scientists collaborated by following a common program and contributed to the development of several thousand geophysical stations throughout the world. The biggest effort was the establishment of bases in Antarctica and the launching of rockets and satellites.

The stations of Antarctica

Eleven countries participated in forming bases in Antarctica—Argentina, Australia, Belgium, Chile, France, Great Britain, Japan, Norway, New Zealand, the United States, and the U.S.S.R. More than forty bases were created (several of them on the Antarctic plateau). Among them were four Soviet stations, two American, and two French.

Loading mica plates at a Siberian air base.

Above: An oil tanker at the American base of McMurdo. *Below:* In McMurdo Bay, launching atmospheric balloons to study the electrical currents of high altitude is common. *Below right:* Flags flown at the South Pole are from countries which collaborated in scientific research in Antarctica.

61

Glossary

adapt to adjust to new environments or situations.

blizzard a long, violent snowstorm with intense, cold winds.

capelin a small northern sea fish related to the smelts.

carnivore an animal that feeds mainly on the flesh of other animals.

continental drift a theory that says that the continents have moved great distances on the earth's surface and are still moving today. According to the theory, the continents once formed a single land mass called Pangaea.

dialect a regional form of a language.

ecliptic the great circle formed by the apparent path of the sun.

Eskimo dog a large dog originally bred in Greenland and Labrador with a thick coat and bushy tail.

fjord a long, narrow, often deep inlet from the sea with steep cliffs on either side.

fletan a type of flatfish found in the Arctic Ocean.

geophysics the study of the physical properties of the earth. This science includes the fields of meteorology, hydrology, oceanography, seismology, volcanology, magnetism, radioactivity, and geodesy.

glacier a large, thick mass of ice moving slowly down a slope or valley, or spreading over a land surface.

Gondwana one of two huge land masses formed when the single land mass, Pangaea, began to split apart. According to the theory of continental drift, Gondwana (or Gondwanaland) formed the continents of Africa, Antarctica, Australia, South America, and the Indian subcontinent.

Günz Glacial the first of four periods of glacier formation during the European Ice Age.

habitat the place or type of site in which an animal or plant can be naturally or normally found.

harpoon a spear with a barbed head used in hunting whales, seals, and large fish.

herbivore an animal that feeds mainly on plants.

ice cap a mass of ice covering a huge area of generally level land and flowing outward from its center.

ice floe a flat, free mass of floating sea ice.

ice shelf a huge platform of ice which rests on the sea.

iceberg a huge floating mass of ice that has broken free of a glacier.

isotherm a line on a chart or map of the earth's surface connecting areas having the same temperature at a given time or the same average temperature over a period of time.

isthmus a narrow strip of land connecting two larger areas.

krouviout an Eskimo term for the thin, soft down of the musk ox.

Laurasia one of two huge land masses formed when Pangaea split apart. According to the continental drift theory, Laurasia eventually formed Eurasia and North America.

magnetic pole either of two nonstationary areas that mark the extremes of the earth's magnetic field. One magnetic pole is found in each hemisphere. Each magnetic pole aligns only roughly with the geographic pole of the same hemisphere.

meteorological stations a base from which the atmosphere and its phenomena can be studied. A meteorological station is especially suited to weather observation and its forecast.

midnight sun the sun above the horizon at midnight in the arctic or antarctic summer.

Mindel Glacial the second period of glacier formation during the European Ice Age.

Northwest Passage a passage by sea between the Atlantic and the Pacific oceans along the northern coast of North America.

Pangaea the single, giant land mass once formed by all of the present continents. According to the theory of continental drift, the earth originally had only one huge land mass. The land mass, called Pangaea, began to break apart 200 million years ago. It originally split into two land masses called Gondwana and Laurasia. As this process continued, it eventually formed the present-day continents.

Panthalassa the single ocean once covering the earth. According to the continental drift theory, Panthalassa was the only ocean surrounding Pangaea.

pinniped any of a group of carnivorous aquatic mammals with all four limbs modified into flippers. Pinnipeds include seals and walruses.

plankton tiny masses of floating aquatic plants and animals found in a body of water.

plantigrade walking on the sole with the heel touching the ground.

plates any of the numerous rigid sections into which the earth's crust is divided.

polynya an area of open water in sea ice.

Pytheas a Greek navigator and geographer of the fourth century B.C., known to have explored the coasts of western Spain, Gaul, and the British Isles.

Riss Glacial the third of four periods of glacier formation during the European Ice Age.

silk route a major trade route for caravans carrying silk, spices, and other rare products from the Orient to India and the Middle East.

sirenian any of a group of aquatic herbivorous (plant-eating) mammals.

steatite a solid form of the mineral talc used in ceramics and insulation.

tabular icebergs gigantic icebergs found in the Antarctic that have a regular shape and flat surfaces. Tabular icebergs are created from the collapsed fronts of huge glaciers and ice shelves.

Viking one of the pirate Norsemen known for plundering the European coasts between the eighth and tenth centuries.

white-out a weather condition in snow-covered areas (such as polar regions) in which no object casts a shadow, the horizon cannot be seen, and only dark objects are visible.

Würm Glacial the last of four periods of glacier formation during the European Ice Age.

INDEX

Adélie penguin, 51
albatross, 52
Amundsen, Roald, 44-45, 46, 58-59
annual ice, 11
anorak, 32
Antarctic Circle, 12
Antarctic Convergence, 49
Antarctic lands, 49
Arctic Circle, 12
arctic lands, 21
arctic tern, 24, 52
atmospheric balloons, 61
auk, 24, 51
autogyro, 59
axis, 8, 11
Baffin, William, 43
Beardmore Glacier, 56, 58
beluga, 17, 40
Bennett, Floyd, 46
blizzard, 11
Borchgrevink, Carsten Egeberg, 54
Byrd, Admiral Richard, 46, 58-59
caribou, 18, 28
carnivore, 26, 53
Charcot, Jean-Martin, 10, 43, 54-55
Columbus, Christopher, 42
continental drift, 6-7
continental islands, 49
Cook, Frederick, 46
crab seal, 53
Davis, John, 43, 54
de Gerlache, Adrien, 54
Dumont-d'Urville, Jules César, 54
ecliptic, 11
emperor penguin, 51
Endurance, 56
Erebus Volcano, 13, 54
Erik the Red, 42
Eriksson, Leif, 42
Eskimo, 30-36
   art, 40
   hunting, 36
   language, 41
   religion, 40-41
Fram, 22
Français, 54
Fuchs, Sir Vivian, 57
geophysical stations, 60-61
geophysics, 60
Gjoa, 44-45
glacier, 14, 22

Glacier, 15
Godwana, 6, 8-9
great auk, 28
Günz Glacial, 8
Henson, Mat, 46
Holm, Gustav, 43
Huron, 54
ice floe, 11, 14, 45
ice shelf, 54
iceberg, 14-15
igloo, 38
International Geophysical
   Year, 60
inuk, 31
ipek, 41
isotherm, 21
Jeannette, 22
kamiks, 32
kayak, 34-35
Land of the Midnight Sun, 12
Lapp, 31
Laurasia, 6, 8
Lema, 44
leopard seal, 51, 53
magnetic poles, 9
maritime islands, 49
matak, 36
meteorological station, 59
midnight sun, 12-13, 45
migration, 31
Mindel Glacial, 8
Mirny, 54
missionaries, 30, 41
musk ox, 27
Nagga Dan, 49
Nansen, Fridtjof, 22, 43
narwhal, 36
Nobile, Umberto, 46
Nördenskjold, A.E., 44
Norge, 46
North Pole, 8, 19-46
Northeast Passage, 44
Northwest Passage, 44
obliquity, 11
Pangaea, 6, 8
Panthalassa, 6, 8
Peary, Robert, 43, 46
penguin, 51, 57
periantarctic islands, 49
petrel, 24, 52
pinniped, 25

plane of the ecliptic, 11
plantigrade, 26
plates, 7
polar animals, 18
polar bear, 18, 26
polar circles, 12
polar fox, 18
polar ice, 11
polar seasons, 11
polar temperatures, 18
poles, 5-18
polynyas, 45
Pourquoi pas?, 43, 54-55
predator, 28, 52
Pytheas, 42
Riss Glacial, 8
Roosevelt, 46
Ross, James, 13, 54
Ross Barrier, 54
Ross Ice Shelf, 54, 58
Ross seal, 53
Saint Brendan, 42
Scott, Robert, 57-58
sea elephant, 53
sea gull, 24
sea lion, 16
seal, 16, 18, 53
Shackleton, Ernest, 56-57, 58
shark, 23
silk route, 44
skua, 24, 51, 52
sled dogs, 39
South Pole, 8, 47-61
Steller's sea cow, 29
tabular icebergs, 15
Terror Volcano, 54
Thule, 42
umiak, 34-35
Vega, 44
Vikings, 42-43
von Bellingshausen, Baron Thadeus, 54
von Humboldt, Alexandre, 60
Vostok, 54
walrus, 25
Weddell seal, 53
Wegener, Alfred, 6, 43
whale oil, 17
white-out, 11
Wilkes, Charles, 54
wolf, 18, 24
Würm Glacial, 8